A GOOD HEALTH GUIDE

Juices That Heal

Natural Health Cures

Maxwell Stein

Juices That Heal
Maxwell Stein

This edition published MMIII by Windsor Group
The Old School House,
St John's Court, Moulsham Street,
Chelmsford,
Essex CM2 0JD

Type set by SJ De sign and Pub lishing, Bromley, Kent

ISBN 1-903904-10-2

Contents

Introduction

Through the ages Man has devised many cures from plants, flowers and other herbs and spices. Countless members of the plant world have healing and health-giving properties, explaining why many traditional and proprietary medicines are still based on earth-grown substances.

Healing plants can be eaten or applied to areas of pain and discomfort or, better still, enjoyed in delicious health-giving teas and juices.

This book is dedicated to just a few of the things Mother Nature offers for Man to convert into healing juices for preventing and treating many common illnesses and complaints.

PART 1

Healing Juice Remedies

ALFALFA

Alfalfa is native to Asia and was transported to other parts of the world sometime in the mid-19th Century. The plant is hardy and highly resistant to drought and disease. It has been cultivated for over 2,000 years and was probably discovered by the Arabs who called it the Father of all Foods. Alfalfa is rich in the organic minerals of calcium, magnesium, phosphorus and potassium, plus most of the known vitamins. It was fed by the Arabs to their horses, in the belief it made them swift and strong.

The English herbalist John Gerard, writing in 1597, records alfalfa as a powerful healing treatment for stomach upsets. The herb is a long-standing healing choice of the North American Indians who use it in medicine for humans and animals.

Scientists say, like other deep-rooted plants, alfalfa is a particularly valuable source of food for Man and animal. But many plant foods stay close to the surface and do not penetrate below the cultivated soil, unlike alfalfa which digs deep into the earth finding minerals in the deep subsoil which other plants miss.

Vitamin U, contained in alfalfa, is believed to heal, even prevent the formation of peptic ulcers. High vitamin K content helps the blood clot properly and protects against haemorrhaging. Alfalfa also has several important enzymes that help promote the chemical reactions necessary to assimilate food in the body.

The plant's benefits for the teeth are acknowledged by leading experts, such as Dr. Sherman Davies of the University of Indiana, who says:" The use of alfalfa as food for humans would be a great boon, and those who produce it will be doing the world a vast service in saving the teeth of all ages." (Source: *Nature's Medicines*).

The medicinal content is in both sprout and leaves, juices of each being used as nutrients and tonic. Alfalfa is a mild diuretic, helping to cleanse the blood and benefit the excretory system. The sprouts are often used during convalescence and general weakness as well as to boost the appetite and help the bowels run smoothly.

Preparation and Selected Uses

☐ Gather the fresh shoots and grind them to a pulp. Add a little water and blend together well. Strain and add a little grapefruit juice to taste.

☐ Alternatively, add a handful of fresh leaves to a cup of boiling water and steep for 5 minutes or so. Strain and store the juice. Again, the taste of neat alfalfa is too strong for most palates, and another, preferably sweeter juice can be added to improve the flavour.

☐ Make a tea from the leaves and drink to relieve painful stomach complaints.

☐ Drink alfalfa tea to reduce water retention and eliminate swelling of the legs and feet.

☐ Alfalfa is believed to treat gangrene in the early stages when consumed as a juice. Benefits are also thought to extend to open sores and runny infections that fail to respond to conventional treatment.

☐ The juice is considered a powerful cure for allergies caused or exacerbated by over-consumption of sugar. Mineral salts contained in the plant make the blood more alkaline and reduce the incidence of allergic reactions.

□ Saponins in the leaves are believed to cleanse the body of fatty plaque on the heart arteries and reduce the threat of coronary disease.
□ Mineral salts in alfalfa, including calcium, magnesium and potassium, are known to benefit the kidneys.
□ A daily drink of the juice treats cystitis and inflammation of the bladder.

Warning

Taken to excess the herb may aggravate lupus and other auto-immune disorders.

APPLE

An apple a day keeps the doctor away. All children know this to be true, and adults, too, will discover the apple is rich in health-giving nutrients and minerals. The fruit is easy to digest and contains solvents, stabilisers, muscle and body builders, oxygen carriers and strengtheners for bone tissue. In the 2nd Century, Galen, a leading court physician, recommended apple wine as a panacea for every known ailment.

The fruit is rich in calcium, phosphorus, iron, sodium, potassium and vitamins. Acids contained in apple neutralise overacidity in the body, explaining why the fruit is commonly taken during fasting and detoxifying. The fruit also helps keep the teeth clean and the bowels moving properly. Organically grown fruits are best.

Apple juice is a favourite medicine of the American Indians who use it to reduce fever.

Preparation and Selected Uses

□ Chop – do not peel – the apple and place in a liquidiser or juicer with a little water added. Blend, strain and bottle the juice.
□ Apple juice helps cure biliousness and is an effective treatment for rheumatism.

☐ Drink apple juice every morning on rising to help ease painful haemorrhoids.

☐ Control increased secretion of urine with regular apple-juice fasts, preferably using organic apples.

☐ Mixed with spinach the juice makes a powerful double treatment, both cleaning the system of toxins and helping to relieve constipation.

☐ Tests on laboratory animals show that apple juice may reduce cholesterol, but only with the pulp included.

☐ Leave apple juice to stand in a warm place for about a week to make your own apple cider vinegar. This is even more beneficial than the basic juice for treating many ailments. This is especially so for arthritis and rheumatism since apple cider vinegar reduces the build up of acid crystal deposits in the joints, known to prompt the disease and cause attacks.

☐ Rose water mixed with apple juice vinegar makes an excellent face wash. Added to bathwater the same mixture helps to reduce fatigue.

APRICOT

Apricot is the common name for a tree of the rose family and its fruit of which more than 20 species exist. The fruit, looking much like a peach, is smaller with a more delicate flavour and is marketed fresh, dried or packaged. The plant is believed to have originated in Central Asia many centuries ago and was later introduced by Romans and Arabs into southern Europe. California and Oregon are the leading US producers and significant crops are grown in British Columbia (Canada), Italy, Australia, Israel and the South of France.

The fruit is a golden bronze colour revealing this as a rich source of vitamin A. Other properties include potassium, phosphorus, calcium, vitamin C and iron.

There is a story about the inhabitants of Hunza Land on the borders of China, Pakistan and the former Soviet Union. Visitors report a youthful looking population even among those in advancing old age.

The country is home to thousands of apricot trees, the fruits of which the natives use in food, confectionery, medicines and cosmetics. The secret of their eternal youth, they say, lies in a diet rich in apricots.

Other fruits and vegetables with high provitamin A or beta-carotene content, including carrots, are gold in colour and present one potential problem, namely that your skin can turn orange if you consume too many.

Preparation and Selected Uses

- ☐ Wash the fruit and remove the flesh. Place in a juicer or blender with 12 fluid ounces of water. Blend until smooth.
- ☐ Fruits and vegetables with high vitamin A content are hailed as major contenders in the fight against cancer.
- ☐ Apricots are high in vitamin A, noted for immense benefits for the eyes. Bodies starved of vitamin A demonstrate common conditions, notably night blindness (inability of the eyes to adjust to darkness); xerosis (where the eyes lack lustre) and sties. All conditions respond very well to continuous treatment with vitamin A.
- ☐ Vitamin A is a very effective treatment for lung conditions caused by excessive exposure to smoke, whether from the patient himself smoking cigarettes or breathing in smoke emitted by others.
- ☐ Vitamin A is essential for the liver to work properly and to resist infection.

ASPARAGUS

The plant probably originated in Europe and Asia long before the birth of Christ, since when it has travelled far and been used extensively in food and medicine. The plant is rich in essential nutrients, including calcium, phosphorus, iron, sodium, potassium, niacin, as well as vitamins A and C.

Asparagus is high in folic acid and is commonly used to treat anaemia, being also thought to help cure renal disorders, acne, eczema and other skin conditions.

Preparation and Selected Uses

☐ Take a handful of the tops and place in a liquidiser or blender to which a cupful of cold water is added. Juice and strain before bottling.

☐ An old Romany medicine for rheumatism involves taking about 26 heads of asparagus cut into tiny pieces and placed in an upper pan with a tablespoonful of water. The pan is covered with aluminium foil and placed in another pan of boiling water and left to simmer for about 4 hours. More water is added as the old liquid evaporates. Then the mixture is left to cool, the upper pan removed and the contents strained through muslin. A tablespoonful of the juice should be taken every 4 hours while the condition lasts.

☐ Chinese herbalists recommend asparagus as an aphrodisiac, being rich in steroidal glycosides that may affect hormone production and stimulate the sex drive.

☐ Asparagus is also used in India to treat infertility and increase milk production in nursing mothers.

Warning

Do not use if the kidneys are inflamed or diseased.

BEET

This ordinary garden plant probably originated in Mediterranean countries, from where it spread to most other parts of the world. The root is most commonly used in medicine, being rich in essential nutrients, including calcium, phosphorus, iron, sodium, potassium, as well as vitamins A and C.

Beet is a powerful body cleanser and an excellent treatment for the liver. Mixed with carrot juice it can be taken to treat anaemia and as a tonic during menstruation.

The juice might offer a treatment for some cancers. According to research carried out all over the world, many sulphur-rich fruits and vegetables – including some spices – have been proved to prevent and treat certain tumours. Red beet root is one of a long list of possible candidates in the race for a cure for cancer. Tests were conducted on laboratory animals inoculated with malignant tumours and administered beet juice. A high proportion of treated animals became cancer-free or lived longer than test animals not receiving the juice.

The juice is believed to treat alcoholism and drug addiction.

Preparation and Selected Uses

☐ Wash the beet but do not peel. Cut into small portions and juice in a powerful machine. Add carrot or pineapple juice to improve the flavour.

☐ Beet juiced with carrot and cucumber in equal parts makes an effective treatment for allergy.

☐ The juice is used in Romany medicine to treat low blood pressure and fight acidity, as well as to control anaemia and keep the blood healthy.

BERRIES

Many berries are healthful, having been used for centuries as food and medicine. Unfortunately, only a handful can be considered in a book of this size.

Berries are rich in potassium, a substance that is believed to prevent or even treat cancer. Potassium is used to control high blood pressure and to help the kidneys function efficiently. For their calcium and phosphorous content, berries help keep the bones and teeth healthy, being also beneficial for the heart and skin.

Berries are rich in iron and calcium, with healthy quantities of vitamin A and C.

BILBERRY

Bilberry, sometimes called huckleberry, has been used in medicine since ancient times mainly for controlling diarrhoea, dysentery and for urinary disorders. Physicians in ancient Greece used a syrup of bilberries to control the flow of milk in nursing mothers.

The berries are rich in vitamins and can be used to treat diarrhoea and nausea. Bilberry has been prescribed for centuries to cure sight deficiencies and as a treatment for eye strain. Jam made from the berries was given to RAF pilots during the Second World War to improve their vision on night flights.

The juice is astringent and germicidal.

Preparation and Selected Uses

☐ Wash the berries and place in a pan of boiling water. Leave to stand for an hour or so then strain and leave the juice to cool before bottling.

☐ If you can afford to, take a handful of berries and leave them to stand for a couple of weeks in a bottle of brandy. The berries release tannin, being the nutrient that helps control diarrhoea. Take a tablespoonful of treated brandy in a small glass of water every couple of hours until the diarrhoea stops.

☐ Wash the berries and liquidise them in a juicer or other suitable machine. The juice makes an effective treatment for dry eczema especially when painted over the area or applied to gauze and left in place until dry. It is also thought to be effective in controlling diabetes.

Warning

The leaves can be poisonous if consumed to excess over a long period.

CRANBERRY

The fruit helps fight infection and is particularly good for cystitis.

Preparation and Selected Uses

☐ Add freshly washed cranberries to a stainless steel pot and fill with pure filtered or distilled water. Simmer the mixture slowly on a low heat for about 10 minutes. Remove and leave the mixture to cool before straining off the liquid. Bottle and take as a soothing drink.

☐ Plentiful drinks of cranberry juice help control attacks of asthma and guard against recurrence.

☐ For asthma sufferers a drink at the onset of the attack can help restore normal breathing.

☐ The berries are high in vitamin C and can help stop bleeding gums.

HAWTHORN

Hawthorn has been used for centuries to treat digestive disorders and insomnia. The berries are rich in bioflavonoids which help strengthen blood vessels and keep the heart healthy. The berries are diuretic, helping to relieve the body of excess water and salt.

Preparation and Selected Uses

☐ Make your own heart tonic by mashing fresh hawthorn berries and drinking 1 part of the juice to 3 parts water.

☐ The juice is believed to help lower blood pressure.

JUNIPER

The berries of the fruit are stimulant and diuretic and contain an oil that is beneficial to the kidneys and can reduce swollen tissues. The berries are used in making gin, juniper being an appetite stimulant; hence gin is a common aperitif. Native Americans use the juice internally and externally to treat arthritis and rheumatism. Indian women also drink the juice as a form of birth control.

Preparation and Selected Uses

- ☐ Crush 1 ounce of the bruised berries in a pint of boiling water. Strain and drink as a juice.
- ☐ To make a tincture, add the berries to vodka or gin and leave to stand for a week or so. Take a teaspoonful of the mixture in water several times a day. The tincture can be applied externally to painful swellings.
- ☐ Rheumatism sufferers should make a strong tea from the needles, wood or bark and add this to their bathwater.
- ☐ Use the juice to bathe haemorrhoids after each visit to the toilet.
- ☐ The berries are highly diuretic and help to relieve water retention.
- ☐ Juice made from the bark can be taken to relieve menstrual pains.
- ☐ A daily drink helps improve the digestion, ease painful gout, and in folk medicine helps to treat problems of the urinary tract.

Warning

Avoid taking juniper berries if you are pregnant or suffer from serious kidney disease.

RASPBERRY

The berries are rich in vitamins B and C. Raspberry contains tannins and is used as a mouthwash to treat inflammation of the mouth and throat. It is also used in eye lotions for conjunctivitis. The fruit is particularly kind to women, for whom it provides relief from menstrual cramps and, taken twice daily as a tea in the later stages of pregnancy, it eases labour and speeds delivery.

Preparation and Selected Uses

- ☐ Clean the berries and liquidise with water to taste.
- ☐ A daily drink helps prevent diarrhoea.
- ☐ Tea made from raspberry leaves is believed to increase supply of breast milk.

- An infusion of the leaves makes an excellent gargle.
- Tea made from the leaves is used in folk medicine to strengthen the uterus and help to prevent miscarriages. The tea is also believed to help ease labour pains.
- After the birth the juice is believed to help the uterus return to normal.
- During menstruation the juice helps relieve painful cramps.

CABBAGE

Cabbage is a biennial herb of the family Cruciferae, growing in temperate regions and used mainly as food and fodder. Related plants Brussels sprouts, broccoli, cauliflower, kale, kohlrabi and Chinese cabbage probably developed from wild cabbage. Cabbage is high in sulphur, an important mineral that gives cabbage being cooked its familiar smell.

Cabbage is believed to be a valuable aid in the fight against cancer, as reported in Cancer Research (May, 1978) and *The Anti-Cancer Diet* (Dr. Donald R. Germann, published by Wideview Books). In the September 1978 edition of Journal of the National Cancer Institute cabbage was listed as a possible anti-cancer food, alongside family members Brussels sprouts and broccoli. Studies carried out recently at the Institute For Hormone Research in New York suggests that several members of the cabbage family – broccoli, cabbage, cauliflower – contain potent anti-cancer chemicals, being rich in indoles, compounds that convert certain potentially lethal oestrogens into benign form.

Preparation and Selected Uses

- Clean the leaves and tear into small pieces before juicing in a liquidiser or juicing machine. The liquid can be mixed with other juices to improve the flavour. We recommend carrots, celery or parsley.

☐ Fresh cabbage juice treats many ailments, including liver and stomach damage prompted by alcoholism as well as peptic and duodenal ulcers caused by excessive alcohol consumption.
☐ Cabbage juice can be used to treat peptic ulcers.

Warning

Over-use of cabbage juice can deplete the body of iodine creating a potential threat to the thyroid gland. Compensate by increasing your intake of kelp or iodine tablets available from health food suppliers.

CARROT

Carrots are rich in vitamins A, B and C, and to a lesser extent vitamins E and K, as well as phosphorus, potassium and calcium.

Regular consumption of the juice helps to cleanse the system of impurities and offers major benefits for numerous eye and skin disorders. Among early American settlers, eye inflammations were treated with carrot juice produced by heating scraped carrots on a fire shovel and later adding hot water. The mixture was cooled and used to bathe sore eyes. The juice was also applied to the breasts to relieve mastitis.

Carrots are believed to lower cholesterol in the body because of their high pectin content, according to Dr. Peter D. Hoagland of Philadelphia's Eastern Regional Research Center, who says: "It may be possible for people with high cholesterol to lower it 10 to 20 per cent just by eating two carrots a day."

Carrots are also used to treat diarrhoea, by replacing electrolytes and minerals escaping from the body through diarrhoea.

Last, but not least, carrot juice helps to keep the skin healthy, dealing effectively with complaints like pimples, whiteheads and blackheads.

Preparation and Selected Uses

☐ Wash the carrots but do not peel. Chop into tiny pieces and juice with a little water added using a fairly powerful juicing machine or liquidiser.

☐ Romany medicine makes ample use of gypsy juice, containing all kinds of fruits and vegetables, according to the condition being treated. One form of gypsy juice treats the body as a whole, helping to keep it functioning properly and aiming to treat all parts. It is made from equal parts of chopped carrot, celery and spinach, mixed with a teaspoonful of chopped parsley. Pour the mixture into a blender or liquidiser and add a cupful of water. Blend to make a drink that is rich in potassium, containing practically the whole range of organic minerals and salts needed to keep the body healthy.

☐ Carrot mixed with beet and cucumber in equal parts makes an effective treatment for allergy.

☐ A daily intake of carrot juice benefits most mild forms of anaemia.

☐ A small portion of carrot juice every day is a useful health-maintaining treatment for the whole family.

☐ Carrot juice served cold or offered warm as a soup is a satisfying meal and can be taken regularly during illness and convalescence.

☐ The juice is believed to reduce cholesterol in the body.

☐ Carrot soup is particularly good for curing infant diarrhoea.

☐ Carrots are rich in beta-carotene, a form of vitamin A that is believed to prevent some cancers. In *The Herb Bible*, Mindell argues: 'Eating one raw carrot a day can reduce your risk of getting certain forms of cancer. Cancer researchers have found that eating 12,500 IU of beta-carotene daily (there are 13,500 IU in one raw carrot) can prevent certain forms of cancer, such as cancer of the oesophagus, stomach, intestines and prostate.'

A study sponsored by the American National Cancer Institute revealed that people whose diets are rich in carrots and other foods containing carotene are less likely to develop certain cancers than those without this essential nutrient in their diet. Surprisingly, the study even recommended that high-risk people, like smokers, might reduce their risk of cancer by eating more carotene.

Warning

One disadvantage might be that over-consumption reveals itself in the colour of a person's skin turning noticeably orange.

CELERY

Celery is the common name for a biennial herb belonging to the parsley family and a native of Europe which now grows throughout the world. Both root and seeds have high medicinal properties being used as carminative, stimulant, sedative, diuretic and tonic.

Stem and fruit have been used for centuries for medicinal and culinary purposes in all parts of the world, for users rich and poor. Celery has been used in China since 5 B.C. and in ancient Egypt it was used to cure diseases cast by demons. Britain's King Henry VIII was an early devotee whose skin was rough and blemished through a diet rich in fatty foods and inadequate vitamins. A court physician decided to test the claims of a skin-purifying herb called smallage – celery – which was pounded and given to the king to drink. Within days the royal complexion improved.

In India a type of celery called ajmoda is used to treat allergies, arthritis and gout, asthma, blood poisoning, bronchitis, cystitis, eczema, hyperactivity, liver and spleen conditions, psoriasis, urinary discharges, rheumatism, hiccough, rectal troubles, flatulence, nasal catarrh and fever. Celery is also used extensively as a sedative or to disguise the flavour of other drugs. In addition, it is considered a powerful aphrodisiac.

The seed is effective against certain types of fungi and is used extensively to treat urinary tract infections because of its powerful antiseptic actions.

Preparation and Selected Uses

- ☐ Wash the stalks and cut into tiny pieces then juice in a liquidiser or juicing machine. Celery juice, though delicious to some palates, is overpowering to others and might be improved by the addition of carrot juice. If this is so, juice the two items separately and mix just before drinking.
- ☐ An infusion can be made by adding 2 teaspoonfuls of the crushed seeds to one cup of boiling hot water. Leave to stand for a few minutes before draining off the seeds and drinking the mixture while still warm.
- ☐ Celery juice is a powerful nerve tonic taken with meals or just before retiring. Seeds and stalk are used in the juice.
- ☐ For a quick and effective tonic, add a teaspoonful of celery salt to a cup of boiling hot water and take as a healing drink to induce sleep and relieve the pain of rheumatism and arthritis.
- ☐ A tonic that is very effective against arthritis and rheumatism is made from vinegar and celery, with Epsom salts and citrus juice added. Mix together half a grapefruit, 1 orange, 1 lemon, 2 sticks of celery and 3 cupfuls of water. Cut the fruit and celery into chunks and simmer in water for about an hour. Press the softened foods and drain. Add 1 tablespoonful each of apple cider vinegar and Epsom salts. Drink a small glassful of the mixture each morning and evening, mixed with cold water or juice to taste.
- ☐ Regular drinks of the juice are believed to increase the flow of milk in nursing mothers.
- ☐ Celery juice can be used to help encourage weight loss as part of a normal calorie-controlled diet.

Warning

Take a maximum 3 cupfuls per day. Do not take during pregnancy. Do not take celery if you are already being prescribed water tablets or taking other diuretics.

CHERRY

The cherry tree is of Asiatic origin and has a long and fascinating history as a healing plant. Pliny tells us the plant was brought to Italy in 68 B.C. by Lucullus. All parts of the tree have been used in medicine and in some countries a juice made from the bark makes a powerful astringent. The American Indians made a decoction of the root which is used to treat many ailments. Cherries are rich in calcium, phosphorus, iron, sodium, potassium, as well as vitamins A and C.

In tests carried out by Dr. Ludwig Blau in the early 1950s, cherry juice was found to be a remarkable treatment for gouty arthritis when: 'no attacks .... occurred on a non-restricted diet in all 12 cases, as a result of eating about one-half-pound of fresh or canned cherries per day'.

The Food Field Reporter (November, 1958) claimed that canned cherry juice offered major benefits for sufferers from arthritis: 'Today, there is no definite scientific data on just how the juice aids in relieving pain caused by diseases where improper balance of calcium is evident. However, it is believed that it may be the pigment in the cherries that brings relief.'

The juice is also very effective at ridding the body of accumulated waste minerals known to aggravate acne.

Wild cherry bark is especially beneficial for sufferers from cold and bronchitis.

Preparation and Selected Uses

☐ Boil the stems of sweet cherries for 2 or 3 minutes, strain and add a tablespoonful of honey. Take as a juice or syrup to control wheezing in colds, influenza or asthma.

☐ Collect cherry bark fresh and release the broken fragments in alcohol or simmering water. Add to water after it has left the boil. Do not allow the bark to boil as this destroys the medicinal value.

Leave the mixture (water based or alcohol) to stand and strain before bottling the juice.

☐ Control palpitations of the heart with regular juice drinks made from the bark of wild cherry.

CHICORY

Chicory probably originated in Europe since when it has spread to most parts of the civilised world. The root is the medicinal part of the plant and is used to treat hepatitis, constipation, water retention and as a tonic for the entire body.

Chicory – called 'tzicory' – is immensely popular in Russian folk medicine and is often taken alone or added to tea or coffee.

Preparation and Selected Uses

☐ The leaves can be chopped fine and used in salads or steeped in hot water for a refreshing tea or juice.

☐ Add 1 ounce of the chopped root to 1 pint of boiling water and leave to simmer for 5 minutes. Strain and bottle the juice or drink hot as coffee.

☐ Take a handful of the early morning flowers and add them to a pint of cold water. Leave to stand in the sun all day. Strain the liquid and store as a juice.

☐ An infusion of the leaves can be used to treat depression and to help reduce water retention.

CUCUMBER

Cucumber is rich in essential nutrients, including calcium, phosphorus, iron, sodium, potassium, and vitamins A and B.

The juice has been used since ancient times to keep the skin healthy and blemish-free. Culpeper himself recommended regular applications to the skin to treat sunburn and lighten freckles.

More recently, Paul Bragg, ardent advocate of cucumber for benefiting the skin, says of the herb in an early issue of *Nature's Path*:

'There is nothing more nourishing for the skin to have than the liquid juice from the cucumber. The nutrition-rich water that it contains, when taken into the body, adds lustre to the hair, sparkle to the eye, colour to the lips, tone to the skin, and spring to the step.'

Cucumber juice is a powerful treatment for arthritis, high blood pressure and rheumatism, as well as helping to prevent constipation. There is evidence that cucumber juice may reduce the pain of insect stings when applied locally. This ability to counteract irritation extends to other problems of the skin, notably poison ivy.

Preparation and Selected Uses

☐ Wash but do not peel the cucumber. Add to a juicer or liquidiser with water to taste. Blend, strain and bottle the juice.

☐ Regular drinks of cucumber juice help fight dry skin and scurvy, taken as a drink or used as a wash for the skin.

☐ Regular drinks of cucumber mixed with beet and carrot in equal parts make an effective treatment for allergy.

☐ Cucumber juice can be added to cotton wool balls and used as a cooling compress for tired eyes. The juice also makes a good skin cleanser and astringent.

☐ The juice can be applied directly to skin irritations for speedy relief.

DANDELION

Dandelion is used in food and drink in many cultures, old and modern, being especially useful for curing gallstones. It is believed to have originated in Asia and is known to have been used by Arab physicians as early as the 10th Century. Dandelion was thought to relieve hypochondria. In France it has long been used to treat chronic skin diseases where it is known as 'dents de lion', an indication of its lion's tooth leaves.

The plant has a fascinating history. During famines on the island of Minorca when all vegetation was stripped by locusts, the inhabitants survived for a long time on dandelion roots, due to their high nutritional content.

Because salts contained in dandelion help to neutralise acids in the blood the plant makes an excellent cleansing tonic. Dandelion is also high in lecithin, a substance that may help protect the liver from cirrhosis.

The leaves are diuretic and contain lots of potassium, calcium, vitamin A and C alongside beta-carotene and iron. The entire plant makes an effective tonic for the liver, digestive system, gall bladder and kidneys. The juice is also taken to cure night blindness, especially juice from the flowers which contains a regenerating substance called helenin. Last, but not least, being rich in vitamin A, the juice is believed to defeat the spread of tuberculosis.

Preparation and Selected Uses

☐ Take leaves from an area that has not been treated with pesticides. Shred the leaves and add to a juicing machine with a little water to taste. Blend and strain before bottling the juice.

☐ Make your own dandelion root coffee by using only freshly gathered roots, washed and left to dry quickly in a warm place. When dried, roast and grind to a fine powder. Add a teaspoonful of the powder to a cupful of boiling water and drink neat or with other herbs to taste.

☐ For a juice made from the tops and flowers take a handful of the plant and add to a pint of boiling water. Leave to stand for ten minutes and strain. A little honey can be added to improve the flavour.

☐ For a juice to treat gallstones take one ounce each of dandelion root, parsley root and lemon balm. Add a half ounce each of liquorice and ginger root and two quarts of boiling water. Simmer until the liquid reduces by about one-half and strain. Take a glass every two hours while the problem lasts but always with advice from your doctor.

☐ Dandelion is a common folk medicine for stimulating the appetite.

- ☐ A tea or juice made from the leaves and flowers is an effective remedy for biliousness, premenstrual water retention and swollen ankles.
- ☐ Drink dandelion tea made from roots or leaves to help reduce urinary tract infections.
- ☐ Dandelion root is a long-standing folk remedy for stimulating a sluggish liver and for relieving constipation.
- ☐ Gypsies treat rheumatism with a daily drink made from 1 ounce of dandelion root simmered in a pint of boiling water for about 20 minutes.
- ☐ Make a juice from the stems and leaves and rub on warts twice a day for 2 weeks or until the problem goes.

FENNEL

The plant probably originated in southern Europe before being transported to most other parts of the world. Fennel is rich in essential nutrients, including calcium, magnesium, potassium, phosphorus, iron, zinc, manganese, vitamin A and some B vitamins.

Fennel has a long-standing reputation as a tonic and is even believed to have aphrodisiacal qualities. Legend tells us the plant was used by the ancients to restore eyesight and to reduce weight.

The plant contains essential oils which give it a strong aroma and mild aniseed flavour that is appealing to most palates. For its pleasant taste fennel was often used to mask the taste of other medicines.

The juice is used to settle indigestion and biliousness and to relieve wind and colic, even in children. Its powerful calming, diuretic and anti-inflammatory properties are used to treat gripe, colic, flatulence and other bowel and intestinal problems. Fennel is a traditional ingredient in babies' gripe water. It is believed to increase the flow of breast milk and is a useful remedy for morning and travel sickness, while also being a natural diuretic. According to early pharmacist Sebastian Kneipp, fennel tea also helps detoxify the body taken as a drink or added freely to bathwater.

The juice is used extensively in folk medicine, taken internally or applied to the skin, to help ease the pain of joints inflamed by arthritis and rheumatism. Sufferers from gallstones are also thought to benefit from a regular intake of the juice.

Fennel is also thought to aid longevity and in ancient times it was thought to offer protection from witches. Bunches of the herb were hung over doors during midsummer to counteract evil spells.

Preparation and Selected Uses

- ☐ Place a teaspoonful of bruised seeds in a stainless steel pan. Pour two cups of boiling water over them and leave to stand for a few minutes. Strain and drink the liquid hot as tea or cold as juice.
- ☐ Take a handful of stems and leaves, rinse thoroughly and liquidise with a little water added. Strain and bottle the juice.
- ☐ Fennel is one of nature's finest remedies for conjunctivitis and other sores and sties around the eyes, the juice being good for bathing and washing purposes.
- ☐ Gypsies use fennel juice to smooth out wrinkles, believing the juice of the leaves and seeds also helps brighten the eyes when applied as a lotion.
- ☐ Tea or juice made from the bruised seeds of fennel is particularly good for relieving gas and helps to regulate menstrual flow.
- ☐ The juice might also be taken during periods of water retention to help urine flow more easily.
- ☐ Fennel has been used for centuries to cure obesity. The usual remedy is a handful of leaves, covered with a pint of water, and left to boil until the liquid is reduced by one half before being strained, bottled and taken as a drink throughout the day.
- ☐ Fennel juice is especially beneficial for treating alcohol poisoning and gout, being effective at reducing toxic waste from the body.
- ☐ Fennel is often used to treat anorexia nervosa.
- ☐ Fennel juice sweetened with honey is a common folk remedy for insomnia.

Warning

Do not use on sensitive skin or just before sunbathing. High doses should be avoided in pregnancy.

GARLIC

Garlic is a long-standing herbal medicine, being used by the ancients to treat many conditions. Dried bulbs were even found in the tomb of King Tutankhamun perhaps as a protection from evil in the afterlife. Culpeper described it as: 'a good preservative against, and remedy for any plague.' (*Complete Herbal*). Hippocrates (460 B.C.) is believed to have used garlic to treat uterine cancer.

The juice has long been used to promote good health and stamina. In the *Home Book of Health* published in 1878, author John Gunn says: 'Garlic is a stimulant, diuretic and expectorant, and applied to the skin, rubefacient, that is, it will produce a blister. The medicinal uses of garlic are very numerous, it being recommended by some as a valuable expectorant in consumption and all affections of the lungs ..... '.

Garlic juice was used through the ages as a means of increasing strength for building pyramids, waging war, getting slaves to work harder, and, as a noted aphrodisiac for promoting quality sex.

The herb contains cleansing, infection-fighting chemicals and essential oils which can be made into a vinegar, oil or juice. The cloves, mashed and diluted with water, were strained and used as a wash for wounds or applied to dressings.

During the First World War, garlic was used externally as an antiseptic. It has even been used to treat leprosy. Taken internally, garlic is used to treat bronchial disorders and is medically proven to reduce cardiovascular problems, including high blood cholesterol.

In Oriental hospitals carrying out organ transplants, garlic is very often the only post-operative antiseptic used. The juice was even tested by Louis Pasteur who found that garlic killed micro-organisms, offering protection against potential killer diseases.

Like other sharp juice roots and bulbs, including onions and masterwort, garlic helps to draw out pain and is believed to restore energy in later life. Garlic syrup is a common folk remedy for controlling asthma.

Growing evidence suggests that garlic can decrease the mortality rate of heart attack victims. At India's Tagore Medical College, researcher Arun Noria monitored over 400 heart attack victims over several years. Half were given garlic juice, the others a garlic-flavoured placebo. Recurrent heart attacks and deaths were dramatically lower for those taking the juice than for those receiving the placebo. Today, garlic is being tested by the American National Cancer Institute in the hope it will finally provide a prevention and cure for the disease.

Ailments garlic treats include: catarrh, colds, colic, hypertension, influenza, rheumatism, warts (applied locally), problems of the colon, and more. Garlic also helps strengthen the immune system.

Preparation and Selected Uses

☐ Make a garlic soup (warmed) or juice (chilled) by mashing and simmering 3 whole garlic clusters. Strain and bottle. Use the liquid mixed with cold water as a soothing juice or added to a can of soup of your choice as a meal.

☐ Peel a handful of garlic cloves and place in a liquidiser or juicer with water added to taste. Juice in the normal way before straining and bottling the liquid.

☐ Rub garlic juice on warts several times a day until the problem goes.

☐ Sufferers from vaginal thrush should include regular drinks of garlic juice in their diet to promote immunity.

☐ Take 4 medium size tomatoes and 2 onions diced into tiny pieces. Add 4 cloves of mashed garlic with a few drops of pure lemon juice and a teaspoonful of vegetable oil. Liquidise with water according to preferred taste and consistency. Take regular drinks.

☐ For a rheumatism liniment, add 4 ounces of garlic juice to 1 quart of apple cider vinegar and ½ ounce of horseradish root. Leave to stand in a warm place for a day or so, shaking the mixture at regular intervals throughout. Strain and bottle the liquid.

☐ Garlic is a particularly good and powerful treatment for catarrh, even for chronic symptoms.

☐ Include ample garlic juice in the diet to help increase the flow of urine and eliminate toxins from the body.

☐ Garlic is good for the heart. Include as much as you can in the diet, preferably as a raw juice. According to a recent article in *Nutrition Review*, garlic and onion are reported to lower serum cholesterol levels and stimulate fibrinolytic activity.

In *The Herb Bible*, Earl Mindell is highly specific about garlic, calling it a 'cholesterol buster which raises HDL (the good cholesterol), lowers LDL (the bad cholesterol) and reduces triglycerides'.

In another study conducted by Dr. Lau of Loma Linda University in California, people with high blood cholesterol were treated to garlic and experienced a fall in cholesterol level of 44 points in six months.

☐ The juice may lead the way in a cure for cancer and heart disease. Researchers say it may even increase the life span of people who have already suffered heart attacks.

☐ For high blood pressure try a daily drink (in several stages if necessary) of 1 pod of garlic and 8 ounces of carrot juice.

☐ Garlic is thought to help prevent blood clots and in countries where curry forms a major part of the diet, the incidence of blood clots is low. The argument is that ingredients in garlic help to stop platelets from combining and forming into blood clots known to cause stroke and heart attack.

Warning

Over-consumption can be toxic and may trigger an allergic reaction. Garlic should be avoided by breast-feeding women: the juice can transfer to breast milk and subsequently cause colic in babies.

GINGER

Ginger is the common name for a plant family having about 50 genera and over a thousand species. The family it belongs to, Zingiberaceae, is parent to other popular spices, like turmeric, cardamom and canna. All members of the family are aromatic – some more than others – and most have been used for centuries for culinary and medicinal purposes.

Ancient records show ginger was used primarily for healing and health purposes before later developing as a flavouring and food. In India, the plant was nicknamed 'The Universal Medicine' or 'Vishwabhesaj'. Ginger is a prime ingredient today in more than half of natural medicines prescribed in the Orient.

It also has a well-founded reputation as a carrier herb, being one that enhances the body's absorption of other health-giving herbs and nutrients.

'Ginger is generally combined with herbs going into the abdominal area, because it is a carrier. Ginger is an herb which accentuates so many herbs.' (Dr. John Christopher, School of Natural Healing, Utah)

The plant has many healing properties, being expectorant, stimulating perspiration, improving digestion and liver function, controlling nausea and vomiting, relaxing spasms and relieving pain. In China, the root (they call it Gan Jiang) is used to treat many conditions, including: uterine bleeding and blood in the urine, coldness associated with shock and chronic bronchitis, mushroom poisoning and dysentery.

In the United States a group of 25,000 doctors, called eclectics, pronounced ginger a miracle healer. Here is a quote from *King's American Dispensatory* by H. W. Felter and J. U. Lloyd, published by Eclectical Medical in 1983:

'When chewed it occasions an increased flow of saliva, and when swallowed it acts as a stimulating tonic, stomachic, and carminative, increasing the secretion of gastric juice, exalting the excitability of the alimentary muscular system, and dispelling gases accumulated in the stomach and bowels ..... It is eminently useful in habitual flatulency, atonic dyspepsia, hysteria and enfeebled and relaxed habits, especially of old and gouty individuals; and is excellent to relieve nausea, pains and cramps of the stomach and bowels ..... especially when those conditions are due to colds ..... Ginger in the form of ginger tea is popular and efficient as a remedy for breaking up colds, and in relieving the pangs of disordered menstruation.'

The plant originated in the East Indies and was brought to Spain in mediaeval times. News of its value – in food and medicine – travelled fast, reaching users rich and poor. Even Britain's Henry VIII pronounced it a cure for many ailments, including the Great Plague.

The plant is also thought to have powerful benefits for sufferers from earache. The Meskwaki Indians were first to notice this, having crushed and simmered the root before using the juice in a poultice on the ears.

The plant helps eliminate parasites from the body and in Japan it is used to treat anisakis, a parasitic infection caused by a diet heavy in sushi or raw fish.

Ginger's benefits for motion sickness are of worldwide renown and in the United States a test conducted on U.S. naval recruits unaccustomed to sailing in heavy seas, concluded that ginger root significantly reduces vomiting and cold sweating normally accompanying travel sickness.

American Indians use an indigenous species to treat infertility and impotence. An old gypsy love potion uses the whole elecampagne plant mashed and added to a handful each of fennel and vervain leaves and a tiny amount of grated ginger. The mixture is warmed in the oven and can be added to wine or water guaranteeing unbridled passion for those who partake of the juice.

Joshua Backon, researcher and writer on ginger, says it might be a cure for impotence due to its ability to offset thromboxane synthetase. As a result, Backon argues this may be the reason why ginger is also an effective treatment for menstrual problems. (*Source: Archives of Andrology, 1988*).

The root is the most important part for juicing purposes, and can be purchased fresh or processed from health shops, grocers and supermarkets.

Preparation and Selected Uses

☐ A nourishing, healing tea can be made by mixing equal parts of dried ginger and hops with hot water. The tea is particularly beneficial for digestive disorders. In India, sufferers from indigestion are treated to ginger tea in place of the regular variety.

☐ See *Honey* for several delicious, health-giving drinks using honey and ginger.

☐ Added to the bath, dried ginger or ginger juice treats many external aches and pains.

☐ A few drops of warmed ginger juice dropped in the ear help reduce painful earache.

☐ The plant is a powerful enemy against parasites, including worms, and can be taken in regular hot drinks throughout the day.

☐ Compresses made from folded cloths dipped in ginger juice or tea and wrung out offer effective treatment when applied direct to the source of pain as in arthritis, rheumatism, muscle tension.

☐ In scientific tests conducted in Denmark researchers found that ginger reversed many symptoms, even of chronic arthritis and rheumatism. In one case, in 1989, patients were asked to consume fresh or powdered ginger for several months, after which all reported fewer symptoms, less pain, and reduced stiffness and swelling than from conventional drugs.

☐ At the time of writing, ginger is a major contender in the fight against cancer. In *Ginger: Common Spice or Wonder Drug?* the author says: 'It is widely believed that environmental exposure to toxins is responsible for as many as 80% of all cancers. When tested against two accepted standards for toxicity, ginger significantly reduced their life-threatening potential.' Ginger, combined with another ancient healer, honey, is believed to hold the key to a cure for cancer.

☐ Ginger is believed to temporarily raise body temperature and promote weight loss.

☐ Take a glassful of the juice before travelling to help prevent or reduce motion sickness.

Warning

Oddly, ginger can have some ill-effects, depending on your point of view. In Jamaica, for instance, it is believed to reduce milk flow in nursing mothers. Much, of course, depends on the mother and her wish, or otherwise, to continue breast-feeding her infant.

HONEY

Honey has a long and fascinating history stretching back thousands of years. For ancient and modern man, honey keeps the body healthy, treats specific ailments, delays aging, increases sexual potency, and promotes general well-being.

'My son eat thou honey for it is good', Solomon says in the book of Proverbs. From the Prophet Mohammed: 'Honey is a remedy for every illness.' More recently Barbara Cartland writes: 'In honey there is contained, I am convinced, the elixir of life. This is the reason why honey is so stimulating to sex, and it is also responsible for its fantastic healing properties.'

Aristotle was one of the earliest believers in the healing powers of honey. Its remarkable energy value has benefited Greek athletes since ancient times. Hippocrates used honey for treating ulcers, a practice that continues in many modern hospitals and clinics. According to a recent *Middlesex Hospital Journal*, honey possesses definite bactericidal properties. Ancient Greek philosophers also believed honey was the Elixir of Youth, maintaining that Man's lifespan could be doubled, given the right combination of foods and nutritional values. Honey came closest to the ideal food.

In *Old Age Deferred*, Dr. Arnold Lorand says: 'As the best food for the heart I recommend honey. Honey is easily digested and assimilated, and it is the best sweet food as it does not cause flatulence and can prevent it to a certain extent, promoting the activity of the bowels.'

Special Note

Honey drinks help cure internal disorders, while neat honey offers quick relief from many external problems.

Preparation and Selected Uses

☐ Honey – clear or set – can simply be added to hot water and stirred until blended.

☐ Basic Mead: Mix 1 part honey with 3 parts water and simmer slowly until the mixture reduces by about a quarter. Allow the mixture to cool and skim off the surface. Pour the remainder into stoneware crocks or dark bottles. Place a towel on top to keep the mixture clean and allow it to breathe. Leave in a cool place. Wait 30 days before tasting. If necessary, leave the mixture a little longer for the taste to develop. Cork and store somewhere cool.

☐ Honey and Ginger Ale (especially good as a digestive aid):
Ingredients: 1 large piece of ginger root, bruised (not powdered ginger) 1pt/600ml boiling water, 1tbsp clear honey, Perrier water to taste.
Method: Put the ginger in boiling water and simmer for twenty minutes. Add honey and leave to melt into the mixture. Put to one side to cool. Add Perrier water to taste.

☐ Julab: Julab derives from the Persian for rose (gul) and water (ab). To make your own take some rose water (from chemists or Indian delicatessens) and mix in a teaspoonful of honey, a few raisins and a couple of pine nuts. Leave to stand for thirty minutes and drink. For a special party drink, float some pretty rose petals in the serving bowl.

☐ Sharaab Health Drink: Sharaab is what most Arabs call alcohol, although the word originally applied to any drink with health-giving qualities. Make your own by adding 1 teaspoonful each of honey and vinegar to a glassful of water.

Honey Cure for Insomnia

☐ Take the juice of 1 lemon and 1 orange mixed with 2 tablespoonfuls of honey in a glass filled with hot water.

Fatigue

☐ Honey and apple cider vinegar mixed with water has been used for thousands of years to replenish energy and fight fatigue. Make your own reviving drink by blending 1 teaspoonful each of honey and apple cider vinegar in a glass of water.
The drink also offers effective relief from arthritis.

☐ Athletes in ancient times consumed honey in food and drinks during training and just before the games began. Even today, many long-distance swimmers and runners take honey for energy and strength.

☐ Second World War pilots on long, dangerous missions during the Battle of Britain, drank honey and water to help fight fatigue.

☐ Sir Edmund Hillary's conquest of Everest was flashed all over the world with a headline quote from his father (a New Zealand beekeeper): 'It's all been done on honey.'

Honey in the Fight Against Cancer

☐ A report in *Science News* (1993) suggests honey may be a prime contender in the fight against cancer. In recent years, a host of studies have identified a broad spectrum of medical attributes in honey – including antifungal, antibacterial, anti-inflammatory, antiproliferative, and cancer-drug-potentiating properties. Now, researchers at the American Health Foundation in Valhalla, N.Y., have uncovered another. In *Cancer Research*, Bandaru S. Reddy and his co-workers describe the ability of honey-derived caffeic esters to inhibit the development of precancerous changes in the colon of rats given a known carcinogen:

'These esters come from the propolis – the brown, resinous, tree-derived material that honey bees use to cement together their hives. Reddy's group considers three derivatives of the caffeic esters promising enough to use in the longer-term animal studies of colon cancer'.

HORSERADISH

Horseradish contains natural antibiotics and is rich in vitamins and essential nutrients, including sulphur and potassium, sodium, calcium, phosphorus, magnesium, copper and vitamins A, B, C and E.

The root has a powerful aroma and tastes much like mustard, being used as a powerful stimulant while also clearing the nasal passages, reducing water retention, and cleansing the body of infection. The juice is also a powerful remedy for swollen tissues (oedema), rheumatism and acne.

Being incredibly strong on flavour and smell, medicines derived from the root can literally bring tears to the eyes, hence horseradish features in the traditional Passover meal to commemorate the plight of the Jews under Pharaoh's rule.

Preparation and Selected Uses

☐ Grate the fresh root and chop into small pieces before juicing in a food blender or liquidiser with a little citrus juice added to taste.

☐ Romany gypsies use horseradish as an antiseptic applied externally to wounds and skin lesions or taken internally as a drink.

☐ For a juice to cure blocked sinuses, take 1 fresh horseradish root, peeled, chopped and juiced with water. Add the juice of 2 fresh lemons and take ¼ cupful of the liquid between meals until the problem goes.

☐ Mixed with honey the juice should be taken several times a day to help cure colds and chesty coughs.

☐ Applied locally the juice helps ease pain and stiffness from arthritis and rheumatism.

☐ For a juice to combat water retention, take 4 tablespoonfuls of freshly grated horseradish root and add 2 cupfuls of apple cider vinegar. Leave to stand for about a day, shaking the mixture regularly. Add 4 tablespoonfuls of glycerine and mix the ingredients. Strain and bottle the liquid and store in a cool place. Drink a tablespoonful of the mixture several times a day. Additionally, use as a regular wash for problem areas.

☐ The juice can help prevent or treat hypothermia, especially in older patients.

Warning

Over-consumption can lead to diarrhoea and excessive sweating.

LEMON

Lemon, being rich in vitamin C, is important for stimulating the brain chemical norepinephrine which is responsible for the body's ability to be alert, attentive and motivated. It takes only a tiny shortage of vitamin C to cause irritability or depression. Citrus fruits have a long-standing reputation for promoting health and curing specific ailments, including scurvy.

The lemon tree originates from the tropical regions of India and Burma where it has grown wild since prehistoric times. The juice improves digestion, cleanses the skin, and helps fight infection, while also being a powerful tonic for the heart and decongestant for the liver.

Scurvy was a common disease among early mariners and led to innumerable deaths. In 1535 Cartier, the French explorer and navigator, became stranded in the Canadian wilderness, having lost one-quarter of his men to scurvy which had seriously weakened the survivors. He and his men lived, thanks to lemon concoctions administered by the Indians from the needles and twigs of an evergreen lemon tree. By the 18th Century, news of lemon's benefits for fighting scurvy spread to all parts of the world and, in England, ships leaving for overseas trips were required by law to carry lemon or lime juice as protection against the disease.

Last, but not least, lemon is believed to contain the secret of eternal youth. At least, that is what early 20th Century German and English doctors believed who recommended that patients drink lemon juice each day to increase their length and quality of life.

The custom of eating a slice of lemon with fish developed for medicinal, not culinary purposes, when it became known that if a bone was lodged in the throat the lemon juice would shift it.

During World War II, British submarine crews were given citrus concentrates as a supplement to their diet. German soldiers, too, were given lemon-pectin powders to sprinkle on wounds to promote clotting. And in Italy, Japan and Germany, the International Red Cross distributed lemon powder to Prisoners of War who diluted it with water to counteract undernourishment.

Preparation and Selected Uses

☐ Slice the fruit in half and extract the juice in a hand-held juicing saucer.

☐ Alternatively, cut the fruit into small pieces and juice in a liquidiser or blender with a little water added.

☐ Boil a lemon slowly for about ten minutes. Slice in two and extract the juice. Add 2 tablespoonfuls of glycerine and take as a syrup for coughs and colds. Alternatively, top the mixture with hot water and take as a regular juice.

☐ Lemon juice mixed with water acts as a sedative and can control nervous palpitations.

☐ Drink a glass of lemon juice and water in equal parts first thing in the morning to beat constipation and purify the blood.

- Regular lemon drinks are useful in controlling some bladder and kidney infections.
- Oil of lemon can be extracted by pulverising the rind and is so strong that a few drops will flavour over a gallon of water.
- A tablespoonful of lemon juice helps cure hiccups quickly.
- Lemon juice rubbed onto the skin lightens freckles and fights blackheads and acne.
- Lemon juice applied to the skin helps relieve irritation from insect bites.
- For heart problems, hardening of the arteries, fragile blood vessels, poor circulation and high blood pressure, a glass of lemon juice each day should bring fast relief.
- In scientific tests conducted at the Florida Southern College, doctors gave lemon peel compounds to rats given cancer transplants and effectively halted the disease. Later tests conducted on humans at the Harlem Hospital in New York revealed that patients taking the lemon treatment were able to withstand much heavier radiation treatment without damage being caused to healthy tissues.
- Smoking is known to deplete the body of vitamin C. Similar effects come from over-consumption of alcohol. Both can be repaired to some extent by increased intake of citrus fruits, especially lemon juice.
- Lemon remedies have been reported in medical books, old and new. Listen to treatments recommended by Drs. Wood and Ruddock in their book *Encyclopedia of Health and Home.*

  Asthma. Many cases of asthma have been relieved by taking a half tablespoonful of the juice of a lemon before each meal and upon retiring.

  Colds and coughs. ..... Dose one-half to a tablespoonful of the juice, sweetened to taste before each meal and again before retiring at night. In severe cases, take it every three or four hours.

  Headache. To the juice of two large lemons add one quart of common table tea, made from the best green tea. Add the juice to the tea when the latter is boiling hot, and when cool bottle for use. Dose, one teacupful, repeated in two or three hours.

☐ Scientific studies in the USA show that senility can be caused by a lack of vitamin C in the diet. This is what it says about the effects of vitamin C deficiency among the aged in *The Key to Good Health – Vitamin C* by Fred R. Klenner, M.D. and Fred Bartz:

'A senile patient is forgetful, confused, his speech rambles. He repeats a question that has just been answered. Memory is so poor the individual does not recognise members of his own family.'

Dr. Berkenau made a study of senile dementia patients at the Warneford Hospital, Oxford, England, in 1940. He found all his patients were short of vitamin C. No exceptions. .....

They quote Dr. P. Berkenau, writing in the *Journal of Medical Science*, saying: 'Plaques appeared in the brain of senile patients identical to those found in alcoholics. This indicates a poisonous origin. Hence senile patients and those approaching old age need substantial quantities of vitamin C to protect their brain from damage and to fight infections.'

☐ Neat lemon juice quickly removes stains from the hands. For teeth discolourations, such as caused by excessive smoking, swirl a teaspoonful of neat lemon juice around the teeth and gums for several minutes before rinsing the mouth clear.

☐ Steep the inner rind of a lemon in vinegar for four hours. Strain and bottle the juice. Use this to bathe warts, repeating the treatment several times a day until the problem clears.

LETTUCE

This very popular salad plant comes from Asia but has been grown in most other parts of the world for centuries. Garden lettuce has been cultivated since the time of the ancient Greeks. In Egypt and China, lettuce has been used for centuries to treat numerous ailments.

Several varieties of lettuce exist, some more health-giving than others. Organic types are recommended, especially romaine which is richer in most essential nutrients than its counterpart, the iceberg lettuce.

It is known that father of herbal medicine, Nicolas Culpeper was an ardent believer in lettuce, especially for curing headaches and nervousness. He took ordinary garden lettuce leaves which were pounded to a pulp and the juice extracted. This was combined with juice from rose petals crushed with a separate mortar and pestle. Having combined the juices, the mixture was smoothed over the forehead and temples and, not only cured the pain, but sent Culpeper into a sound sleep.

Other treatments founded on lettuce are to cure coughing and treat insomnia.

Preparation and Selected Uses

☐ Use all the leaves of the lettuce since the outside leaves which we normally discard, are richer in nutrients than those towards the centre. Rinse the leaves to remove dirt and juice in a liquidiser or juicing machine.

☐ Romany medicine employs lettuce tea as a treatment for insomnia. The recipe involves taking the outside leaves of a large lettuce and adding them to a sauce pan containing half a pint of boiling water. A little salt is added and the mixture left to simmer for twenty minutes before being strained and the juice left to cool. Gypsies drink a glassful of the juice last thing at night to promote sleep and rid the system of impurities.

☐ To treat sunburn, boil a handful of leaves and strain the juice. Leave to cool and store in a refrigerator. Dip a cotton wool ball into the mixture and apply to areas of pain.

MELON

Melon is a common name for members of the gourd family, including winter melon, watermelon, muskmelon and cantaloupe. Muskmelons have a soft, ribbed rind and distinctive salmon coloured pulp. In America these are frequently referred to, wrongly, as cantaloupes. Winter melons have harder rinds and are less aromatic than muskmelons and include popular varieties honeydew, Persian, casaba and Crenshaw. The true cantaloupe grows mainly in Europe, having hard, warty skins with deep grooves. Watermelons vary in shape, size and markings, varying from round to oval, and ranging from dark through to light green, sometimes with stripes. The flesh is usually red and deliciously sweet.

CANTALOUPE

Cantaloupe is particularly beneficial for health and comes with a hard rind and sweet tasting orange flesh. It is high in nutritional content, including calcium, phosphorus, iron, sodium and several vitamins.

Cantaloupe itself treats several illnesses including Crohn's disease characterised by a narrowing of the bowel and upset stomach, especially of the digestive tract. Cantaloupe is rich in beta-carotene and other natural sugars and enzymes having a laxative effect on the colon.

Preparation and Selected Uses

☐ Take a ripe cantaloupe and cut it in half. Remove the seeds and wash the inside of the melon. Peel it and cut into tiny sections before blending or liquidising.

WATERMELON

Watermelon is a popular harvest of the South American Indians who grow several varieties and use the fruit for food and medicine. Pueblo Indian tribes consider the melon so precious it is commonly given as gifts on ceremonial occasions.

Watermelon is useful for treating patients after major surgery or when convalescing from illness. Among American Indians it is used to treat many ailments of infant and elderly tribe members.

It is particularly useful for treating skin conditions, especially eruptions caused by poor diet. The juice of the watermelon is effective for flushing acid from the body and renewing the blood.

Preparation and Selected Uses

☐ Cut the melon in half and remove the seeds. Wash the fruit and peel. Cut into sections and juice or blend.
☐ Seeds from the watermelon can also be infused in tea and used to treat urogenital complaints.

MUSTARD

Mustard is the common name for a large family of herbs usually grown for food and including other salad and vegetable crops such as cabbage, cauliflower, Brussels sprouts, broccoli and kohlrabi.

The plant has been used since Roman times as a digestive tonic and laxative. Culpeper prescribed mustard juice applied locally to ease sciatica and taken as a juice with honey for curing coughs and colds.

Mustard leaves look a bit like kale but a little lighter colour. Essential nutrients in mustard greens are especially beneficial for women and help to supply calcium needed to keep muscles and bones healthy and strong. High vitamin A content is beneficial to vision, teeth, hair and skin. Mustard greens treat painful menstruation, rheumatism and sciatica.

Preparation and Selected Uses

☐ Remove the stem and midribs from the leaves and rinse to clean. Juice in a standard juicing machine or liquidiser.
☐ Add the juice to a footbath and use it to soak the feet for as long as the water is hot. This helps to stimulate the circulation and warm the entire body.
☐ Mustard powder or juice added to bathwater or a footbath helps relieve colds and flu.

Warning

Prolonged use can cause irritation.

NETTLE

The most common member of the family Urticaceae is Urtica Dioica, the stinging nettle. The leaves are rich in essential minerals and vitamins, including calcium, phosphorus, iron, sodium, potassium, and vitamins A, C and P.

Nettle has been used for centuries for healing and medicinal purposes. The early Romans took the plant with them on their travels in colder climates, using it to flog their limbs to counteract the cold and pain. The American Indians also use nettle as a counter-irritant for pain by striking the affected parts with prickly branches. They also made a decoction of the root to bathe rheumatic pains and stiffness of the joints.

Nettle is the basis of many folk remedies for hayfever and other allergies and may help to relieve inflammation caused by allergic reactions, as in the nose and chest.

A recent study carried out at the American National College of Naturopathic Medicine found that 57 per cent of patients treated with nettle derivatives experienced substantial relief from allergy symptoms.

Nettle is an excellent styptic, checking the flow of blood almost as soon as administered as a poultice. It seems that all parts of the plant are serviceable, even the stems which can be made into linen.

In *Vitalogy* (1925), Drs. G. P. Wood and E. H. Ruddock say: 'For haemorrhages the express juice of the fresh leaves is regarded as more effective than the decoction, given in teaspoonful doses every hour or as often as the nature of the case requires.'

As a drinking juice, nettle treats arthritis, diarrhoea, dysentery, eczema, piles, neuralgia and inflammation of the kidney. There is growing evidence that it also treats dropsy in the early stages. Other uses include helping to promote the flow of milk in nursing mothers and as a wash to help the hair grow. For external use the juice can be used to bathe minor wounds and grazes.

It is also a nutritional food and not unpleasant taken as a cooked vegetable or made into soup. Even Hippocrates considered the nettle a valuable vegetable food.

Russian herbalists have used nettle in medicines for hundreds of years, as an antiseptic, astringent and blood purifier. In animal tests the plant has been shown to lower blood sugar levels, indicating a possible treatment for diabetes.

Preparation and Selected Uses

☐ Two teaspoonfuls of dried nettle leaf can be added to a cup of boiling hot water and left to stand for a few minutes before being strained and consumed as tea or juice.

☐ Rinse a handful of nettle leaves and place in a blender or liquidiser with a little water added to taste. Blend then strain and store the juice in an airtight container.

☐ Minor cuts and grazes can be treated with an external application of nettle juice.

☐ Regular intake of the juice might help prevent cardiac oedema and water retention.

☐ The plant is particularly beneficial for women, helping to treat menstrual cramps and heavy blood flow. It is useful for treating vaginal infections such as candida.

☐ For a hair tonic and treatment for dandruff, mix 4 tablespoonfuls of crushed nettle leaves in a cup of boiling water. Leave to stand until cool before straining and massaging into the hair and scalp.

☐ Regular drinks of nettle juice help relieve painful gout.

☐ Drink nettle tea sweetened with honey to treat neuralgia.

Warning

Nettle juice should be consumed in moderation. Excessive intake can be dangerous, especially of uncooked leaves.

ONION

Onion offers enormous healing benefits used internally or externally. Taken internally, the juice stimulates the body and improves the circulation. It can be applied externally to sprains, bruises and unbroken chilblains.

The herb was widely used by the ancient Romans and Egyptians and probably existed several centuries before. The early American settlers used onion juice mixed with honey as a treatment for nagging coughs. Culpeper prescribed onion to help an inveterate cough and expectorate tough phlegm.

Over the centuries the pungent aroma and taste of onions have been used to ward off witchcraft and plague, being hung over doors to stop evil and illness entering the home.

Onion and garlic juice have been proved to reduce cholesterol levels taken after a fatty meal. According to British medical journal, *The Lancet:* 'Both garlic and onion juices have now been found very significant in preventing fat-induced increase in serum cholesterol and plasma fibrinogen ..... They may prove to be a convenient and safe dietary measure for everyday use in persons who appear to be predisposed to atherosclerosis on account of family history, hyperlipemia, hypertension, or diabetes.'

A drug derived from onions is a powerful disinfectant helping to relieve catarrh as well as soothing sore eyes and painful earache. Applied to the scalp the juice is believed to ward off baldness.

Preparation and Selected Uses

☐ Remove the skin and chop the onion into small pieces. Place in a liquidiser or juicer with a little water added and juice in the usual way.

☐ To unblock the sinuses, juice some fresh onions and inhale the vapours.

☐ Fresh onion juice can be used to bathe the skin to help relieve bruises and sprains.

☐ Applied several times a day to stubborn warts the juice is one of the most effective treatments of all.

☐ Rub the juice into the skin to relieve athlete's foot.

☐ Apply the juice locally to help fade liver spots and other dark blemishes.

☐ An early English folk remedy uses fresh onion juice to bathe haemorrhoids.

☐ For stuffy colds and flu, take a cupful of onion juice and add a small cabbage leaf. Bring to the boil and simmer for 5 minutes. Remove the leaf and add a little honey to taste. Drink as hot as possible while the condition lasts.

PARSLEY

Parsley is a member of the Mediterranean plant Umbelliferae and is believed to originate from Greece. The root is the most important part for medicinal purposes, although leaves and seeds have essential applications, too. The plant is rich in vitamins and minerals, including vitamins A, B and C, calcium, iron and potassium. This last ingredient is thought to hold possibilities for preventing cancer, given that cancerous cells may be unable to multiply in potassium.

Parsley has a long and fascinating history stretching back thousands of years, having been used in funeral rites by the ancient Greeks and in ancient Rome as a tonic to increase the strength of gladiators. Mixed with honey, it has been used for centuries to sweeten the breath, especially after consuming garlic. The juice was once used to lighten freckles and to cure epilepsy.

American Indians drink parsley juice to relieve renal congestion and to treat inflammation of the kidney and bladder, as well as for eliminating gravel, stones and excess water.

Russian folk medicine uses parsley – Petrushka – in teas and juices, being administered for dropsy, indigestion, liver and spleen complaints and prostatitis. Applied to the skin the juice is a powerful non-toxic insect repellent.

Parsley is also used to treat cellulitis, mercury poisoning, rheumatism, skin problems, renal congestion, inflammation of the kidney and bladder, kidney stones and bloating. It is also thought to treat most types of allergy, including sneezing from contact with dust and other airborne substances.

The herb is used as an aid to digestion and is a natural diuretic helping to resolve most cases of mild water retention, such as during menstruation, also being useful for treating cystitis, thrush and vaginal disorders. Parsley cools the blood and soothes the nerve centres of the head and spine.

Parsley is health-giving benefits have been recognised for years as many books and research papers testify. In *Mon Herbier de Sante* (by Maurice Messegue, published by Laffont/Tchou 1975) the author says: 'You should gorge yourself on it (parsley), in salads, omelettes, in soups, as a juice and with all of your meat dishes.'

Preparation and Selected Uses

☐ Wash a handful of parsley and drain before juicing in the normal way. The juice itself tastes good even if some prefer it combined with other flavours such as carrot or celery.

☐ Add a teaspoonful of dried parsley to a cupful of boiling water and stir continuously for several minutes. Strain and bottle the juice after cooling.

☐ Scrape a handful of fresh parsley roots and leaves and crush. Immerse in cold water and bring to the boil. Simmer for 5 to 10 minutes and remove from the heat. Leave to cool. Strain and take as a juice to relieve prostatitis.

☐ A cupful of parsley juice each morning is a good way to keep the skin clear and healthy and is particularly beneficial for treating pimples and rashes. The juice can also be used as a wash for problem skin.

☐ Parsley juice can be used to rinse the urinary organs after each visit to the toilet, being especially useful for treating cystitis and vaginal thrush. But the juice has benefits for gentlemen, too, who will also benefit from using it to bathe the penis after urinating.

☐ Parsley has strong deodorising properties and is especially beneficial when the juice is added to bathwater.

☐ The juice has a toning effect on the uterus and can be used to ease painful labour.

☐ Being highly diuretic, the juice helps remove excess fluids and waste from the body, and can aid weight reduction.

Warning

Do not take during pregnancy. The seeds are poisonous if consumed in quantity.

PEPPERMINT

This is a favourite taste of people all over the world taken either as confectionery or in soothing teas and juices. Peppermint is good for the digestive system, helping to control diarrhoea and spasms, as well as relieving indigestion. It is particularly good for treating motion sickness and small portions of the juice should be carried at all times when travelling.

Peppermint has been popular through the ages, for medicinal and cosmetic purposes. The ancient Greeks and Romans sprinkled the crushed leaves in their wine or mixed it with honey as a means of disguising bad breath. Early American Indians used tea made from peppermint as a cure for most stomach problems, while the early settlers used it for dyspepsia. In Jamaica, peppermint tea is used to treat colic.

The leaves are rich in tannins and essential oils, including menthol, having strong antiseptic qualities. The plant is used extensively in treatments for colds and chesty coughs. Other medical applications include digestive upsets, morning sickness, flatulence, colic and diarrhoea.

Peppermint juice can heal headaches quickly and bring speedy relief from muscle cramps. As a wash, the juice treats areas of pain, such as stomach pain and headaches.

Preparation and Selected Uses

☐ Add 1 teaspoonful of the dried herb to a cupful of boiling water and leave to steep before straining and storing the juice.

☐ Stress headaches often respond to peppermint juice taken at the onset of an attack or immediately the pain has appeared.

☐ The juice can be heated and used as an inhaling mixture to treat migraine and headaches, especially with sinus complications.

☐ Peppermint tea or juice offers quick relief from blocked sinuses and can be added to a large, warm piece of cloth and applied over the area of pain while the patient lies resting.

☐ Peppermint tea offers speedy relief from sickness, especially caused by travel.

☐ The tea is stimulating and helps clear the head and mind. It is commonly taken before exams to aid mental clarity.

Warning

Not to be taken internally during pregnancy or by people with sensitive skin.

PINEAPPLE

The pineapple family consists of 2,000 species in 46 genera, growing mostly in the tropics and subtropics of America, with one species occurring in western Africa. The plant is believed to originate from

Brazil and today is grown commercially in most tropical areas having the right climate and soil: Central America, Hawaii, The Philippines, Mexico and Taiwan.

Pineapple juice is used in treatments for:

☐ Phytobezoar. This is a type of ball that forms in the stomach after gastrointestinal surgery, being a gastric pile-up of vegetable fibres, starch and fat.
☐ Enzyme dysfunction.

Preparation and Selected Uses

☐ Pineapple is one of the easiest fruits to juice, with or without a juicing machine. Without a machine, simply cut the fruit into slices and squeeze manually until all of the liquid is removed. With a juicer, remove the thorny outer skin and chop the fruit into small pieces before liquidising with a little water added.
☐ Pineapple juice is a powerful aid to reducing and preventing gastric problems and can be taken at every meal. It is particularly beneficial with a tiny amount of papaya juice added.

Warning

Because of its high sugar content, the juice may be unsuitable for some people, such as sufferers from diabetes or hypoglycaemia.

POMEGRANATE

This is the common name given to a small tree or thorny shrub of the pomegranate members of the family Punicaceae. The fruit is round, about the size of an orange and filled with seeds. The fleshy seed coats are sweet if not also slightly acid-tasting. The astringent rind of the fruit is used in medicine and in tanning.

Although native to semi-tropical Asia, pomegranates are now grown extensively throughout the Mediterranean region. In North

America pomegranates are grown commercially south of California and Arizona.

The ancient Egyptians used the fruit in cosmetics believing it to benefit the skin and keep it from aging. The fruit featured extensively in ancient religious and artistic circles, being described in the earliest of Asian literature. King Solomon sings in the *Old Testament* of 'an orchard of pomegranates' and archaeologists have discovered many graves from Solomon's time at Tel Nami in Israel where sceptres have been found bearing symbols of the fruit. Earrings shaped like pomegranate blossoms were discovered close by. Ancient sites in Iraq also unearthed signs of the fruit being symbolically used in animal sacrifices.

Pomegranate juice is thought to benefit the heart even where extremely weak. Israeli doctor, Dr. Ben-David calls it his 'liquid mouth-to-mouth resuscitator', meaning that even where the heart is weakening, the juice may support consciousness longer than might otherwise be so.

The juice is used in the Middle East as a gargle for halitosis caused by yeast infection, rotting teeth or throat infections. Intestinal worms are treated in Egypt and other parts of the Near East with regular drinks of pomegranate juice. The juice is thought to paralyse the worms and prompt evacuation.

Preparation and Selected Uses

☐ Pomegranate is difficult to eat in its natural state, being heavy in seeds and pith, and with a tough, obstructive rind. The fruit is best juiced whole, that is unpeeled. Cut the fruit into small pieces and liquidise by the preferred method. Strain the juice before serving.

☐ Low blood pressure may respond to treatment with pomegranate juice.

☐ The high astringent content is beneficial when applied to haemorrhoids on cotton wool balls.

POTATO

The potato is an edible tuber produced by certain plants belonging to the nightshade family of which the white potato is the most common. It is grown throughout the world, mainly for food.

Freshly unearthed potatoes contain 78 per cent water, 18 per cent starch, 2 per cent protein, 1 per cent ash, and a tiny proportion of fat. The best part of the potato, for health purposes, is the skin, oddly the part most people remove and discard.

The potato, as most people know, originated in the Americas and was introduced to Europe in the 15th and 16th Centuries. The earliest known users were South American Indians who called the plant papa and used it as food and medicine.

The juice can be used to treat blackheads and other skin eruptions, to treat sinus problems, and to remedy gallstones and bed sores.

Preparation and Selected Uses

☐ Wash the potato but DO NOT remove the skin. Chop into small pieces and liquidise in blender or juicer. A little water may be needed to improve the consistency for drinking.

☐ Boil a large pan of potatoes and drain off the juice. Use the juice hot as an inhaling mixture for treating sinus congestion.

☐ Once the heads of blackheads, boils, carbuncles and cysts are lanced, a paste of potato juice and pulp can be applied to a tiny piece of clean cloth and left to dry over the eruption.

☐ Daily intake of raw potato juice is highly effective for treating gallstones.

☐ Treat bed sores, wounds and leg ulcers to a potato pulp compress.

☐ Potato juice drinks are a good way to keep the skin healthy. Drink at mealtimes and at the start of every day.

PUMPKIN

Pumpkins originate from Central and South America where the juice has been used by Hopi and Zuni Indians to treat leukaemia with apparent success.

Pumpkin has been used for healing purposes for centuries. In China the fruit is the symbol of health, being known as 'Emperor of the Garden'.

The seeds hold valuable healing properties having been used in folk remedies for centuries for expelling tapeworm and correcting urinary disorders. In the *Dictionary of Materia Medica* by Merat and De Lens, mention is made of pumpkin seeds being used to expel tapeworms without fail.

In 1820, Cuban doctor, M. Mongeney, published his findings from using the flesh of pumpkin to treat tapeworms and other internal parasites, relating that he had found the remedy quite by accident and found it to be consistently good. He recommended patients to fast in the morning and somewhere about midday to take 3 ounces of fresh pumpkin reduced to a juice. An hour later 2 ounces of honey was administered.

In 1851, the *Boston Medical and Surgical Journal* directed attention to the healing powers of pumpkin juice in combating tapeworm. The juice was also listed in the *Dispensatory of the United States, 1894*, as 'one of our most efficient and harmless taeniafuges' (a remedy for expelling tapeworm).

The juice of the seeds is a common and long-standing folk remedy for problems of the prostate gland. It is interesting to note that in countries where pumpkin is commonly eaten the incidence of prostate trouble is far lower than among people not used to this delicacy.

The juice is rich in beta-carotene which is easy to digest and gives the liver a major boost. Pumpkin juice is of major benefit to sufferers from vitamin A deficiency, being rich in this particular vitamin. It is also highly beneficial in treating allergies, skin problems, vision disorders, infections, swollen joints, lung and liver problems.

Preparation and Selected Uses

☐ Peel the outer casing and remove the seeds. Cut into portions and juice in a heavy juicing machine designed for tougher substances.
☐ Pumpkin is an effective treatment (internal and external) for swollen joints.
☐ The juice can be used to bathe a smarting burn.

RADISH

Radish is the common name for a family of herbs belonging to the mustard family of which the most common type is the garden radish. The plant is thought to originate from China, now being common throughout the North Temperate Zone. Varieties differ in shape, size and colour, depending mainly on the growing season. Radishes can be purchased with their tops intact or removed. For juicing purposes, radishes with greens intact are best.

An inscription in Egyptian characters on a pyramid records the quantity of radishes, onions, and garlic consumed by labourers who constructed it.

Radish is believed to be a major benefit for the thyroid gland. In *Food is Your Best Medicine* the author, Henry G. Bieler, M.D., lists numerous benefits of a diet rich in radish, mainly for its effects on the thyroid and treatment of obesity. Thyroxine (T4) is essential to bodily functions of cell production, heart beat and repair of body tissues, among others. Raphanin, the main sulphur content of radishes maintains production of thyroxine and other hormones essential to proper functioning of the thyroid.

Radish juice is used to treat constipation, fatty liver disease, inflammation of the gall bladder, as well as thyroid conditions, hypothyroidism and hyperthyroidism.

Preparation and Selected Uses

☐ Always use freshly harvested radishes with leafy tops intact. Cut into tiny pieces to make juicing easier. Add a tiny amount of water and juice in a juicing machine or liquidiser.

☐ Radish is a common folk remedy for gallbladder inflammation and for treating underactivity.

☐ Radish juice is a particular favourite of Romany gypsies who use it to purify the blood and for treating digestive disorders.

RHUBARB

The plant originated in Tibet and was grown in monastery gardens all over Europe for its mild astringent and purgative actions.

Rhubarb is the common name for members of herbs belonging to the buckwheat family of which there are about 50 species native to Asia. The plant has strong, fleshy roots. The stalks are mainly used in cooking, often for preserves and pie fillings.

A medicinal rhubarb from China is a common ingredient for many proprietary American herbal medicines. Rhubarb is extremely beneficial for removing plaque and tarter and for treating many diseases of the teeth and gums.

That said, however, excessive use of rhubarb has side-effects. The raw juice contains high amounts of oxalic acid as William H. Lee advised in *The Book of Raw Fruit and Vegetable Juices and Drinks:* 'Rhubarb is not a friend to Man; I was tempted to leave it out of my book altogether .....' To compensate many proprietary herbal medicines using rhubarb contain just the right amount and recommended dose.

The juice can be used as a poultice or wash for external conditions or taken internally for others, including bedsores, constipation, diarrhoea, gangrene, haemorrhaging, intestinal gas, intestinal parasites, leg ulcers and wounds.

Preparation and Selected Uses

☐ Chop the stalk into tiny pieces and blend in a juicing machine. Alternatively, look for a ready-prepared recipe in health food shops.

☐ For external application make a paste out of a teaspoonful of rhubarb juice and ¼ teaspoonful of honey. Apply to bedsores, ulcers and wounds.

☐ For internal consumption, take a small glass containing 1 part rhubarb juice to 3 parts warm water.

☐ Powdered root can be added to hot water and taken as a juice to relieve stomach and bowel troubles.

Warning

The leaves are poisonous to humans and aphids. A mixture of leaves and hot water can be left to stand before being strained and used as an insecticide.

SPINACH

Spinach is high in vitamins and minerals and has been used in folk medicine for centuries, being thought to reduce the incidence of birth defects and miscarriages. For modern Man the high iron content of the juice helps treat anaemia, being particularly beneficial for women whose need increases during menstruation. The juice is also thought to benefit the skin and to help stop wrinkles forming.

Preparation and Selected Uses

☐ Wash fresh spinach leaves under cold water and shake to remove excess moisture. Add the leaves to a juicer or liquidiser with half a cup of water to taste. Blend in the usual fashion before straining and bottling the juice.

☐ Dip a cotton wool ball into the juice and apply in a circular motion to the skin around the eyes, across the forehead and around the corners of the mouth, wherever wrinkles are known to form. Do this each morning and night to help prevent wrinkles and to reduce any that are already present.

STRAWBERRY

Strawberry is a member of the Rosaceae family, being highly prized for its beauty and delicious-tasting fruit. Leaves, root and berries are used in medicine and have a mild astringent and diuretic effect.

Culpeper describes tonic made from the leaves being used to 'cool the liver and blood and assuage all inflammations of the veins and bladder, provoke urine, and allay the heat and sharpness thereof.'

Strawberry leaves are an effective treatment for eczema. Leaves or root are used to treat adults and children suffering from arthritis and gout, constipation, diarrhoea, dysentery, problems of the urinary organs, water retention, and as a general all-over tonic. The juice used as a gargle strengthens the gums. In Russia, strawberries, called 'Zemlianika', are prized as a highly effective diuretic.

Preparation and Selected Uses

☐ Add one teaspoonful of fresh or dried root or leaves to a cupful of boiling hot water and steep for 15 minutes before straining.

☐ To juice, take whole strawberries and add them to the liquidiser or juicer with a little water added to taste. Take with every meal to help ease painful gout.

☐ Boil a handful of strawberry leaves and leave to simmer for 5 minutes before straining. The juice can be used to treat mild dysentery.

☐ Make your own mouthwash by boiling strawberry leaves in water. Strain and store the juice in an airtight container and use regularly throughout the day.

☐ Juice made from the leaves can be used as a lotion on minor burns and for bathing cuts and grazes.

☐ The undiluted juice of crushed strawberries is a centuries-old recipe for fading freckles.

☐ Strawberry juice, sipped and passed around the teeth and gums, will whiten the teeth.

☐ An infusion of the leaves helps reduce fevers and makes an effective gargle for fighting infection.

Warning

Some people are unable to tolerate strawberries and may be affected by skin rashes and redness.

WATERCRESS

Watercress is a member of the mustard family native to Europe but now grown throughout the world, usually in moist banks and running waters. Watercress is mostly used as a garnish, as in salads, but also makes a delicious, extremely health-giving juice. The leaves are rich in many essential nutrients, including calcium, phosphorus, iron, sodium, potassium, vitamins A, C and E, and magnesium.

The early American Indians used the herb to treat liver and kidney conditions, and to dissolve kidney stones. It was highly prized by the ancient Romans, too, who considered it a powerful treatment for people whose minds were disturbed.

J. E. Myers of the Botanical Gardens of Indiana, USA, tells us that watercress is one of the very best sources of vitamin E. Tests reveal that dried watercress contains three times as much of the vitamin as is present in lettuce leaves.

Preparation and Selected Uses

☐ For an infusion of the fresh or dried herb, add one teaspoonful to 1 cupful of boiling water. Steep for 5 minutes and take three or four times a day.

ZUCCHINI

Zucchini is another name for courgette which others call green squash. The plant originated in Italy and is a popular delicacy throughout the world.

The fruit is rich in sodium which Dr. Henry G. Bieler author of *Food Is Your Best Medicine* (Random House, 1966) refers to as: 'The most ideal source of refurbishing a sodium-exhausted liver'. Legendary starlet, Gloria Swanson, is reputed to have taken zucchini squash to combat chronic fatigue successfully.

Other treatments based on zucchini include those for calcium malabsorption, fractures and osteoporosis.

Preparation and Selected Uses

☐ Wash the fruit but do not peel. Cut into pieces lengthwise and juice in the normal way with a little water added to taste.

PART 2

Additional Juices and their Uses

Avocado

Avocado belongs to the sunflower family and is believed to cure numerous ailments, including obesity and overweight (the juice helps reduce desire for fattening tastes), chronic fatigue and diabetes. Dry skin and scalp conditions can be treated with avocado juice along with problems of malnutrition and underweight.

According to scientists, the seed contains antibiotic substances, being the basis for treating many conditions. Peel the avocado making sure not to cut into the flesh and leaving the outer membrane just beneath the peel intact. Blend with a little water or tomato juice.

Chervil

Ancient herbalists used chervil as a tonic for the blood and nerves and as an aid to improving the memory. Today it is employed mainly as a tonic and aid to digestion, helping also to restore the appetite.

Fig

Fig juice helps fight constipation and has been used for drawing boils since ancient times.

☐ Use fig juice to hasten a boil. Stand an opened fig in half a cupful of hot water and remove the fruit after 10 minutes or so. Bathe the boil with the juice. For boils on the gums use the liquid regularly as a mouthwash. Four tablespoonfuls of fig juice added to a cupful of hot water makes an effective gargle which should last for several days.

Kelp

Kelp is a seaweed from which many essential nutrients come. It is high in vitamins and minerals and is particularly rich in calcium and iron. Additionally, it contains iodine as needed for efficient functioning of the thyroid.

Kelp has been used to treat obesity and to help ease rheumatic pains and ward off gout.

☐ An infusion can be made using 2 teaspoonfuls of the dried plant added to a cupful of boiling water and left to stand for five minutes before straining the mixture and taking as a drink.

☐ Taken as a drink the plant helps to protect the thyroid gland and to prevent goitres.

☐ Regular drinks of kelp juice keep the body healthy and help fight infection.

Pea

Pea is the common name for a subfamily of herbs belonging to the family Leguminasae and probably originated in Egypt several centuries B.C. Two main varieties grown for their seeds are common (garden) pea and the field pea. The fruit is a pod containing seeds.

Medicinal benefits of pea juice include the treatment of celiac disease, constipation and irritable bowel syndrome. Pea juice is most beneficial served warm, like a thin soup.

☐ Wash a cupful of peas and juice in a liquidiser or juicer to which half a cupful of cold water may be added if desired.

Rosehip

The berries are mildly laxative, being rich in tannins and containing lots of fruit acids, especially citrus.

☐ Boil some rosehips in vinegar and use the juice to bathe areas of gout and rheumatism.

Tomato

Helps prevent chronic fatigue and fights yeast infection.

☐ Wash but do not peel the tomatoes and juice in a liquidiser or blender with a little water included. Strain before bottling the juice.

PART 3

Ailments and their Juice-Based Cures

Many more juice cures are available than those included in earlier pages of this book. Most can benefit the condition taken internally or applied to areas of pain.

Abdominal Pain

Selected Juice Therapy: Citrus fruits, ginger.

Aches and Pains

Selected Juice Therapy: Ginger, honey.

Acne

Selected Juice Therapy: Asparagus, Brussels sprout, carrot, cherry, garlic, green vegetables, horseradish, kelp, lemon, onion, raspberry, spinach, watercress.

Aging

Selected Juice Therapy: Apricot, honey.

AIDS

Selected Juice Therapy: Chilli pepper, pumpkin

Alcohol Abuse

Selected Juice Therapy: Beet, cabbage, fennel.

Allergy

Selected Juice Therapy: Alfalfa, beet, carrot, celery, cucumber, honey, nettle, parsley, pumpkin, spinach.

Anaemia

Selected Juice Therapy: Apples, beet, carrot, cherry, dandelion, honey, raspberry, spinach, tomato, watercress.

Anorexia

Selected Juice Therapy: Fennel, gooseberry.

Antiseptic

Selected Juice Therapy: Honey.

Anxiety and Anxiety Attacks

Selected Juice Therapy: Fennel, honey.

Aphrodisiacs

Juice Solutions: Artichoke, asparagus, ginger, honey.

Appetite (loss of)

Selected Juice Therapy: Alfalfa, Brussels sprout, chervil, dandelion, juniper.

Arteriosclerosis

Selected Juice Therapy: Avocado, garlic, onion.

Arthritis

Selected Juice Therapy: Alfalfa, apple, avocado, carrot, celery, cherry, cucumber, dandelion, fennel, garlic, ginger, honey, juniper, nettle, strawberry, watermelon. Grapefruit juice can be taken where it does not aggravate the stomach.

Asthma

Selected Juice Therapy: Carrot, celery, cherry, cranberry, citrus fruits, garlic, grapefruit, honey, potato, turnip, watercress.

Astigmatism

Selected Juice Therapy: Beet, carrot, celery, cucumber, parsley, spinach.

Athlete's Foot

Selected Juice Therapy: Onion.

Backache

Selected Juice Therapy: Pomegranate, strawberry.

Baldness

Selected Juice Therapy: Carrot, celery, garlic, horseradish, lettuce, mustard, onion, radish.

Bed Sores

Selected Juice Therapy: Honey, kohlrabi, potato, radish, rhubarb.

Bed-Wetting

Selected Juice Therapy: Honey.

Biliousness

Selected Juice Therapy: Carrot, celery, honey, parsley, spinach.

Blackheads

Selected Juice Therapy: Lemon, potato, strawberry.

Bladder Problems

Selected Juice Therapy: Alfalfa, beet, carrot, cucumber, lemon, parsley, spinach.

Blood (miscellaneous problems and conditions)

Selected Juice Therapy: Alfalfa, apple, cabbage, cauliflower, celery, cucumber, lemon, lettuce, okra, spinach, tomato, turnip, watercress.

Blood Clots

Selected Juice Therapy: Garlic, pea.

Blood Poisoning

Selected Juice Therapy: Celery.

Blood Pressure

Selected Juice Therapy: Beet, carrot, cucumber, garlic, hawthorn, honey, parsley, pomegranate, spinach.

Boils

Selected Juice Therapy: Beet, carrot, cucumber, fig, garlic, honey, lettuce, nettle, potato, strawberry, turnip, watercress.

Breasts and Breast-feeding

Selected Juice Therapy: Celery, raspberry.

Breathing Tract Problems

Selected Juice Therapy: Honey.

Bronchitis

Selected Juice Therapy: Beet, carrot, celery, cherry, citrus fruits, cucumber, turnip, watercress.

Burns

Selected Juice Therapy: Garlic, ginger, honey, onion, pumpkin, strawberry.

Cancer (prevention of)

Selected Juice Therapy: Apricot, beet, cabbage, carrot, garlic, ginger, honey, lemon.

Carbuncles

Selected Juice Therapy: Potato, strawberry, turnip, watercress.

Cardiac Oedema

Selected Juice Therapy: Nettle.

Cataract

Selected Juice Therapy: Bilberry, honey.

Catarrh

Selected Juice Therapy: Garlic, onion.

Cellulitis

Selected Juice Therapy: Parsley.

Chicken Pox

Selected Juice Therapy: Elderberry.

Chills

Selected Juice Therapy: Ginger.

Cholesterol

Selected Juice Therapy: Apple, cabbage, carrot, garlic, onion, pumpkin.

Circulation (problems of, poor, sluggish)

Selected Juice Therapy: Garlic, mustard, raspberry.

Colds and Flu

Selected Juice Therapy: Cherry, citrus fruits, garlic, ginger, honey, mustard, onion, raspberry.

Colic

Selected Juice Therapy: Fennel, peppermint, watermelon.

Colitis

Selected Juice Therapy: Banana, honey.

Complexion

Selected Juice Therapy: Carrot, gooseberry, olive, parsnip, papaya.

Conjunctivitis

Selected Juice Therapy: Apple, carrot, celery, fennel, orange, spinach.

Constipation

Selected Juice Therapy: Alfalfa, apple, apricot, beet, cantaloupe, chicory, cucumber, dandelion root, fig, grape, honey, lemon, lettuce, orange, pea, prune, radish, raspberry, strawberry, tomato, watercress. A diet rich in fruit and raw vegetable juices is a major benefit.

Convalescence

Selected Juice Therapy: Watermelon.

Coronary Disease

Selected Juice Therapy: Alfalfa.

Coughing

Selected Juice Therapy: Fennel, fig, garlic, honey, lemon, lettuce, onion, parsley.

Cramps

Selected Juice Therapy: Honey.

Cuts

Selected Juice Therapy: Nettle, persimmon, strawberry.

Cystitis

Selected Juice Therapy: Alfalfa, bilberry, celery seed, garlic, parsley, passion fruit.

Cysts

Selected Juice Therapy: Potato.

Dehydration

Juice Solution: Papaya.

Detoxification

Selected Juice Therapy: Ginger, honey.

Diabetes

Selected Juice Therapy: Artichoke, bilberry, cabbage, carrot, celery, chilli pepper, parsley, spinach.

Diarrhoea

Selected Juice Therapy: Blueberry, apple, carrot, celery, ginger, honey, nettle, parsley, peppermint, radish, raspberry, rhubarb, spinach.

Digestive Problems

Selected Juice Therapy: Dandelion leaf and root, fennel, ginger, honey, peppermint, pineapple.

Dizziness

Selected Juice Therapy: Gooseberry.

Drug Addiction

Selected Juice Therapy: Beet, stringbean.

Drunkenness

Selected Juice Therapy: Honey.

Dysentery

Selected Juice Therapy: Blueberry, citrus fruits, nettle, strawberry leaves.

Ears (abscess, ache, bony growths in, itching, tingling, wax in)

Selected Juice Therapy: Elderberry, ginger, onion.

Eczema

Selected Juice Therapy: Asparagus, blueberry, celery, elderberry, nettle, strawberry.

Emphysema

Selected Juice Therapy: Turnip, watercress.

Energy (lack of)

Selected Juice Therapy: Honey.

Exertion (recovery from)

Selected Juice Therapy: Honey.

Exhaustion

Selected Juice Therapy: Honey.

Eyes and Vision

Selected Juice Therapy: Apricot, carrot, dandelion, fennel, bilberry, pumpkin.

Fatigue

Selected Juice Therapy: Apple, avocado, grape, honey, raspberry, spinach, tomato, zucchini.

Fatty Liver Disease

Selected Juice Therapy: Radish.

Fever

Selected Juice Therapy: Cantaloupe, elderberry, honey, peach, pear, raspberry.

Flatulence

Selected Juice Therapy: Fennel, ginger, peppermint.

Fungus

Selected Juice Therapy: Celery, garlic, onion.

Gallstones, Gall Bladder (aids to health of)

Selected Juice Therapy: Dandelion, radish.

Gargling

Selected Juice Therapy: Honey, parsley, strawberry.

Gastric Food Ball

Selected Juice Therapy: Peppermint, pineapple.

Gastritis

Selected Juice Therapy: Banana, plum and prune.

Germs (fight against)

Selected Juice Therapy: Honey.

Gingivitis

Selected Juice Therapy: Rhubarb, strawberry.

Glands (aids to health of, disorders of, swollen)

Selected Juice Therapy: Bean Sprout.

Glaucoma

Selected Juice Therapy: Bilberry.

Goitre

Selected Juice Therapy: Carrot, celery, kelp, parsley, spinach.

Gout

Selected Juice Therapy: Alfalfa, blueberry, carrot, celery, cherry, cucumber, elderberry, juniper, kelp, nettle, rosehips, spinach, strawberry, watermelon.

Haemorrhages

Selected Juice Therapy: Alfalfa, apple, carrot, celery, nettle, radish, spinach.

Haemorrhoids

Selected Juice Therapy: Apple, juniper, nettle, onion, persimmon, pomegranate.

Halitosis

Selected Juice Therapy: Carrot, celery, cucumber, lemon, parsley, pomegranate, spinach.

Hangover

Selected Juice Therapy: Honey.

Hayfever

Selected Juice Therapy: Beet, carrot, celery, cucumber, honey, parsley, spinach.

Headaches

Selected Juice Therapy: Beet, carrot, celery, cucumber, ginger, gooseberry, honey, lettuce, peppermint, spinach.

Heart (aids to proper function of, dilated, diseases of, murmurs, constriction of muscles, palpitations, weak, pain)

Selected Juice Therapy: Alfalfa, asparagus, beet, carrot, celery, cherry, garlic, grape, hawthorn, honey, horseradish, lemon, nettle, onion, parsley, pomegranate, spinach.

Heartburn and Indigestion
Selected Juice Therapy: Banana, dandelion leaf or root, fennel, ginger, peppermint, watermelon.

Hernia
Selected Juice Therapy: Carrot, celery, parsley, spinach.

Hiccups (cures for)
Selected Juice Therapy: Honey, lemon.

Hot Flushes
Selected Juice Therapy: Ginger, honey.

Hyperactivity
Selected Juice Therapy: Celery.

Hypothermia
Selected Juice Therapy: Horseradish.

Hysteria
Selected Juice Therapy: Fennel.

Impotence
Selected Juice Therapy: Ginger, honey.

Infection (chronic, protection against)
Selected Juice Therapy: Honey, kelp, pumpkin, strawberry.

Infertility
Selected Juice Therapy: Honey.

Inflammation (of adenoids, of eyes, ligaments, lungs, nasal membrane, ribs, urinary bladder)
Selected Juice Therapy: Honey.

Insomnia

Selected Juice Therapy: Fig, fennel, hawthorn, honey, lettuce, passion fruit, peppermint.

Insulin Shock (diabetic)

Selected Juice Therapy: Honey.

Irritability

Selected Juice Therapy: Honey.

Irritable Bowel Syndrome

Selected Juice Therapy: Pea, peppermint.

Jaundice

Selected Juice Therapy: Gooseberry.

Joints (aids to health of, pain in, tenderness of)

Selected Juice Therapy: Ginger, pumpkin.

Kidney Stones

Selected Juice Therapy: Blueberry, parsnip, raspberry.

Kidneys (aids to health of, burning in, diseases of, pain in)

Selected Juice Therapy: Alfalfa, asparagus, dandelion, lemon, nettle, parsley, watercress.

Labour Pains

Selected Juice Therapy: Raspberry leaves.

Laryngitis

Selected Juice Therapy: Apple, beet, carrot, celery, cucumber, ginger, honey, pineapple.

leukaemia

Selected Juice Therapy: Pumpkin.

Liver (aids to health of, sluggish, tumours of)

Selected Juice Therapy: Apples, apricot, beet, carrot, celery, chervil, cucumber, dandelion, grapefruit, lemon, parsley, prune, pumpkin, tomato, watercress.

Malaria

Selected Juice Therapy: Bilberry, citrus fruits.

Malnutrition

Selected Juice Therapy: Avocado, honey.

Measles

Selected Juice Therapy: Elderberry, ginger.

Menopause

Selected Juice Therapy: Ginger, honey.

Menstruation (problems of)

Selected Juice Therapy: Beet, ginger, honey, juniper, mustard, nettle, raspberry.

Migraine

Selected Juice Therapy: Ginger, honey.

Miscarriage

Selected Juice Therapy: Raspberry leaf, spinach.

Morning Sickness

Selected Juice Therapy: Ginger, honey, peach, pear, peppermint, raspberry.

Mumps

Selected Juice Therapy: Elderberry.

Muscles (soreness in, twitching of, ache in)
Selected Juice Therapy: Ginger, honey.

Nausea and Vomiting
Selected Juice Therapy: Apricot, citrus fruits, ginger, honey, lemon.

Nerves (aids to health of, centres and malnutrition of, disorders of, exhaustion, injuries to, irritation of, tonic for)
Selected Juice Therapy: Beet, carrot, celery, cucumber, honey, lettuce, onion, parsley, spinach, turnips.

Nervous Tension
Selected Juice Therapy: Honey, lettuce.

Neuralgia
Selected Juice Therapy: Honey, nettle.

Night Blindness
Selected Juice Therapy: Carrot, dandelion.

Obesity
Selected Juice Therapy: Avocado, artichoke, celery, fennel, ginger, honey, kelp, parsley.

Osteoporosis
Selected Juice Therapy: Zucchini.

Palpitations
Selected Juice Therapy: Cherry, honey, lemon.

Parasites
Selected Juice Therapy: Ginger, honey, onion, pomegranate, pumpkin, radish.

Pleurisy

Selected Juice Therapy: Beet, carrot, celery, cucumber, parsley, pineapple.

Pneumonia

Selected Juice Therapy: Citrus fruits, turnip, watercress.

Poison Ivy

Selected Juice Therapy: Cucumber, elderberry.

Pollen (sensitivity to)

Selected Juice Therapy: Honey.

Prostatitis

Selected Juice Therapy: Parsley, pumpkin.

Psoriasis

Selected Juice Therapy: Celery.

Rash

Selected Juice Therapy: Blueberry.

Rheumatism

Selected Juice Therapy: Apple, asparagus, celery, cherry, cucumber, dandelion, fennel, garlic, ginger, grape, grapefruit, juniper, horseradish, leek, mustard, nettle, rosehip, tomato.

Rickets

Selected Juice Therapy: Apple, carrot, celery, orange, spinach.

Sciatica

Selected Juice Therapy: Mustard greens.

Second-Hand Smoke

Selected Juice Therapy: Apricot.

Senility (prevention of)

Selected Juice Therapy: Honey, lemon.

Sex Glands (aids to proper functioning of)

Selected Juice Therapy: Ginger, honey.

Sinuses (disorders of)

Selected Juice Therapy: Horseradish, kholrabi, onion, potato.

Skin (aids to health of, treatment of disorders, dry, eruptions, itching, parchment-like)

Selected Juice Therapy: Apple, asparagus, avocado, carrot, celery, cherry, cucumber, gooseberry, honey, horseradish, kelp, mustard, olive, parsley, potato, pumpkin, strawberry, watermelon.

Sores

Selected Juice Therapy: Alfalfa, honey.

Spleen (disorders of, pain in)

Selected Juice Therapy: Celery.

Stomach (aids to health of, acid, disorders of, gas in, ulcers)

Selected Juice Therapy: Alfalfa, garlic, grapefruit, honey, lemon, peppermint, pineapple, radish.

Stroke

Selected Juice Therapy: Bilberry.

Sunburn

Selected Juice Therapy: Cucumber, honey, lettuce.

Swelling (in abdomen, ankles, eyes, feet, glands, liver, testicles, toes, etc.)

Selected Juice Therapy: Alfalfa, celery.

Tartar

Selected Juice Therapy: Rhubarb, strawberry.

Taste (abnormal)

Selected Juice Therapy: Parsley.

Teeth (aids to health of, decay, sensitivity to cold)

Selected Juice Therapy: Alfalfa, apples, rhubarb, strawberry.

Thyroid (aids to health of)

Selected Juice Therapy: Kelp, radish.

Tonsils (disorders of, tonsillitis)

Selected Juice Therapy: Citrus fruits, elderberry, passion fruit.

Travel Sickness

Selected Juice Therapy: Ginger, honey, peppermint.

Trembling

Selected Juice Therapy: Honey.

Tuberculosis

Selected Juice Therapy: Dandelion, turnip, watercress.

Ulcers

Selected Juice Therapy: Alfalfa, cabbage, celery, ginger, honey, raspberry.

Underweight

Selected Juice Therapy: Honey.

Urinary Tract Infection

Selected Juice Therapy: Cranberry, dandelion, juniper.

Urination (burning, frequent, help in, disorders)

Selected Juice Therapy: Mint, parsley, strawberry, watermelon.

Vaginitis

Selected Juice Therapy: Nettle, parsley.

Varicose Veins (treatment of)

Selected Juice Therapy: Bilberry, persimmon.

Vomiting

Selected Juice Therapy: Citrus fruits.

Warts

Selected Juice Therapy: Garlic, lemon, onion.

Water Retention

Selected Juice Therapy: Alfalfa, celery, chicory, dandelion, horseradish, juniper, nettle, parsley, strawberry.

Weak Heart

Selected Juice Therapy: Pomegranate.

Weakness

Selected Juice Therapy: Honey.

Whitlows

Selected Juice Therapy: Turnip, watercress.

Whooping Cough

Selected Juice Therapy: Fig, turnip, watercress.

Wrinkles

Selected Juice Therapy: Cucumber, fennel, honey, spinach.

Yeast Infection

Selected Juice Therapy: Raspberry, tomato.

Bibliography and Recommended Reading

Ginger: Common Spice or Wonder Drug? by Paul Schulick, published by Herbal Free Press, Brattleboro, Vermont (USA, 1995)

Nature's Medicines by Richard Lucas, published by the Parker Publishing Company Inc. (USA, 1966)

The Herb Bible by Earl Mindell, published by Vermilion (UK, 1994)

A Handbook of Natural Remedies for Common Ailments by Linda A. Clark, published by Pocket Books Inc. (USA, 1976)

Arthritis and Folk Medicine by D. C. Jarvis, published by Pan Books Ltd. (UK, 1962)

Back To Eden by Jethro Kloss, published by Longview Publishing (USA, 1939)

Better Health Through Natural Healing (Thorsons, USA/UK, 1985 and 1987)

Common and Uncommon Uses of Herbs for Healthful Living by Richard Lucas, published by Parker Publishing Co. (USA, 1969)

Dr. Goodenough's Home Cures and Herbal Remedies by Dr. Josephus Goodenough, published by Crown Publishers Inc. (USA, 1982)

Dr. Homola's Natural Health Remedies by Samuel Homola, published by Parker Publishing Co. Inc. (USA, 1973)

Everybody's Guide To Nature Cure by Harry Benjamin, published by Thorsons

Folk Medicine by D. C. Jarvis, published by Pan Books Ltd. (UK, 1961)

From Eden to Aquarius: The Book of Natural Healing by Greg Brodsky, published by Bantam Books (USA, 1974)

Health Secrets of Plants and Herbs by Maurice Meseque, published by William Morrow and Co. (USA, 1975)

Herbal Medicine: The Natural Way to Stay Well by Dian Dincin Buchman with The Herb Society, published by Tiger Books International (UK, 1991)

Herbs by J. and S. Hopkinson, published by Cassell (UK, 1990)

Herbs by Roger Phillips, published by Pan Books Ltd. (UK, 1990)

How to Enjoy Better Health from Natural Remedies by Bernard Jensen, published by Bernard Jensen Publishing (USA, n.d.)

Natural Folk Remedies by Lelord Kordel, published by Manor Books (USA, 1974)

Nature Cure for Constipation and Other Bowel Disorders by Harry Clements, published by Thorsons Publishers Ltd. (UK, 1968)

Nature Has a Remedy (It Can be Physical, Mental or Spiritual) by Bernard Jensen, published by Unity Press (USA, 1978)

Nature's Healing Agents by Swinburne Clymer, published by Humanitarian Society (USA, 1905)

Nature's Medicines by Richard Lucas, published by Wilshire Book Company (USA, 1969)

Rodale's Encyclopedia of Natural Home Remedies by Mark Bricklin, published by Rodale Press (USA, 1982)

Science of Herbal Medicine by John Heinerman, published by Bi-World Publishers (USA, 1979)

The Complete Book of Natural Medicines by David Carroll, published by Summit Books (USA, 1980)

The Healing Power of Herbs by May Bethel, published by The Wilshire Book Co. (USA, 1972)

The Miracle of Garlic by Paavo Airola, published by Health Plus (USA, 1978)

Using Plants for Healing by Nelson Coon, published by Hearthside Press (USA, 1963)

The Doctor's Book of Home Remedies by the editors of Prevention Magazine Health Books, published by Rodale (UK, 1994)

Indian Herbalogy of North America by Alma R. Hutchens, published by Merco (USA, 1973)

HEALING
TEAS

Introduction

Anyone with a small garden or window box can grow their own herbs for making into herbal teas and juices. If you don't have space to grow herbs or you just don't want to, herbalists can supply all of your needs, either by you visiting their premises or by approaching any of a wide selection of mail order suppliers.

Tea is a particularly convenient and pleasant way to take natural medicines and can be made from almost any root or herb, tasting delicious and offering enormous healing and restorative properties. Yet still we rely on supermarket tea for quenching the thirst when our gardens and hedgerows are positively packed with alternative ingredients.

Habit and convenience of use is the main reason drinkers think tea always comes in packets, from leaves picked and processed in China, India and Ceylon. In fact, centuries before the advent of supermarkets, these countries actually imported sage for making tea because the taste was superior to indigenous teas.

Making Tea

Generally speaking, herbs used in tea should be infused, not boiled. The process is similar to making ordinary tea, where leaves are placed in the teapot and boiling water added. Unless otherwise stated, the usual formula is one ounce herb, flowers, leaves or root, as appropriate, to one pint of boiling water. Warm the teapot first, add the herb, and pour on water after it has stopped boiling. Stir well and leave the mixture to stand according to preferred strength.

Adder's Tongue

The plant belongs to the lily family. Bulb and leaves are used in medicines, sometimes combined with horsetail grass and made into tea which is used internally to treat bowel disorders and as an external wash for tired, inflamed eyes.

Simmered in milk the fresh root and leaves make a health-giving tea for sufferers of dropsy, and to relieve hiccups and vomiting.

Juice extracted from the leaves and bulb, mixed with apple cider vinegar, can be used in place of the tea.

Externally, the fresh leaves, bruised and juice extracted, can be applied to ulcers and tumours.

Preparation: One teaspoonful of the dried leaves or root should be added to one cupful of boiling water. Leave to cool before straining. Take warm or cold. One cupful can be taken each day, in regular small doses.

Agrimony

The plant has a long and fascinating history as a medicinal herb, of which John Parkinson *(Theatre of Plants, 1640)* said: 'made with wine, is good against the sting and biting of serpents'.

Harold Ward, writing in *Herbal Manual* (1936) says of the herb: 'Agrimony is an old remedy for debility, as it gives tone to the whole system.'

Externally, the tea can be applied to expel thorns and splinters from the flesh.

Preparation: Make the tea by adding a pint of boiling water to one ounce of the herb and leave to stand for five minutes before straining and serving. To improve the taste, add a little honey or pure maple syrup.

Alder

The medicinal part, the bark, has tonic and astringent qualities and can be used to treat jaundice, diarrhoea, gangrene, dropsy and other debilitating illnesses.

The bark should be aged before use as in its green state it can induce vomiting. In folk medicine, juice from the berries is mixed with apple cider vinegar and given to children suffering from worms. It is often rubbed into the scalp to relieve the discomfort of head lice and to kill the parasites.

Externally, tea and juice can be used to treat ulcers and most skin conditions.

Ale Hoof

The leaves are the medicinal part, which are used as a stimulant and tonic to ease stomach-ache and excess gas. Mixed with honey the tea makes an excellent gargle especially for sore throats and mouth ulcers. The fresh juice boiled and used as an inhalation brings fast relief from stubborn headaches.

The plant has a long history in folk medicine and ancient herbalists believed it could cure insanity and melancholia.

Externally, tea or juice can be applied locally to wounds and grazes.

Preparation: One teaspoonful of the herb to one cupful of boiling water left to stand for several minutes.

Alfalfa

Alfalfa is one of the oldest known healing herbs, being used by ancient Arabs who dubbed it 'father of all foods'. Sixteenth-century herbalist, Gerard prescribed it for upset stomachs and other digestive disorders.

As one of the most robust herbs – it is highly resistant to drought and disease – its roots delve deep into the ground searching for moisture.

The sprouts are highly nutritious as food especially for convalescents.

Organic salts contained in alfalfa are among the richest known. The leaves are the medicinal part and are used to treat numerous conditions, being a good overall tonic. Ancient and modern athletes use alfalfa for increased energy and endurance.

Tea made from the leaves is an effective treatment for stomach complaints and a popular treatment for constipation. It is often used to treat infections of the urinary tract. It is also a common folk remedy for bloating and swelling caused by rheumatism.

Alfalfa is a useful diuretic and helps cleanse the body and improve overall tone. Soak the legs and feet in warm water with alfalfa tea added to help reduce swelling and bring fast relief to arthritis and rheumatism.

Alum Root

The medicinal part is the root, which has a powerful astringent taste and is used to treat diarrhoea. Boiled root water is used in folk medicine for general debility and as a treatment for fever.

American Indians applied the fresh juice to sores and swellings and as a lotion to soothe tired eyes.

Externally, the cooled tea can be used to treat conditions where the skin is cracked and as a gargle for mouth and throat. Internally the tea is administered to patients suffering from diabetes, diarrhoea and dysentery.

Preparation: Add a quarter of a teaspoonful of powdered root to each cupful of boiling water and leave to stand in the teapot for several minutes. Strain and drink hot, warm or cold. One cupful can be taken each day in regular small doses.

Amaranthus

The name comes from the Greek meaning 'unfading', explaining why the flowers of some species stay fresh-looking long after they are picked and dried. The medicinal parts, the flowers and leaves, are astringent and are taken as tea or juice to treat excessive menstruation, diarrhoea and dysentery.

Juice or tea can be used as a gargle to treat painful mouth and throat conditions and can be applied externally to lesions.

Preparation: Make the tea from one teaspoonful of the plant steeped in a cupful of boiling water. Leave to stand until cool and take a cupful throughout the day.

Angelica

The plant is said to be named after the Archangel Raphael who appeared as a vision to a tenth-century monk, during which he pronounced angelica as a cure for the plague.

Over the centuries the plant has developed a reputation as an aphrodisiac with seemingly greater effects on women than on men, explaining why, in the eighteenth century it was a common treatment for frigidity.

In ancient times, tea made from roots, leaves and seed was taken as a treatment for nervous exhaustion, epilepsy, hysteria, and by patients suffering from indigestion, heartburn, stomach-ache and bloating.

Culpeper himself prescribed the plant, alleging: 'It helpeth the pleurisy, as also all other diseases of the lungs and breast.'

The tea is a good digestive aid and evidence suggests the plant may also have potential for treating anorexia nervosa because it helps stimulate the appetite. Root, herb and seed are used in folk medicine particularly as a hot tea to treat stubborn colds, flatulent colic and heartburn.

The tea can be used as a lotion on external ulcers and as a regular drink to relieve menstrual pain. Rubbed over areas of pain it provides fast relief from swelling caused by rheumatism.

Preparation: Make tea from one ounce of the seed or herb steeped in a pint of boiling water and leave to stand until cool. Take a cupful several times a day.

Aniseed

In ancient Rome the tea was used to sweeten the breath while also being considered a powerful aphrodisiac.

Soaked in milk the herb makes a tasty tea believed to induce sound sleep. Milk flavoured this way is used in many parts of the world as an antidote to drunkenness and hangover.

In ancient and modern folk medicine it is believed to increase the flow of milk in nursing mothers. A recent study at Auburn University in the USA reveals that cows sprayed with anise oil produced more milk than cows not receiving the treatment.

The tea is a good decongestant for blocked nose and sinuses. Regular drinks help clear colds and influenza, and also relieve wind and digestive disorders.

Arnica

Rhizome and flowers are the medicinal parts, which can be dangerous if consumed to excess. The flowers contain essential oils with a strong smell and taste and possess antibiotic and antiseptic properties.

The liquid – spirits or infusion – can be applied as a lotion or compress to rheumatic joints, bruises, painful swelling and tired limbs. As tea taken sparingly it helps reduce coughing. Some claim the tea can be rubbed into the scalp to help promote hair growth.

WARNING: Not to be taken internally except under medical supervision. Do not apply to broken skin. Some herbalists believe the herb is too powerful for prolonged use. Mindell *(The Herb Bible)* suggests an overdose can even be fatal.

Preparation: Spirits of Arnica can be made by adding brandy or medicinal alcohol to the flowers. Leave for three or four days and use five drops as a tincture every three or four hours.

To make tea add two teaspoonfuls of flowers to a cupful of boiling water, simmer for ten minutes and leave to cool. Take in five-drop amounts, reduced dosage for children.

Balmony

The leaves are the medicinal parts of the plant, which produce a bitter tonic that has a longstanding place in folk medicine. Tea made from the leaves is used to treat jaundice, chronic malarial complaints, dyspepsia and constipation. Regular doses help to expel worms and other intestinal parasites.

Preparation: Make tea from one teaspoonful of dried or fresh leaves to each cupful of boiling water. Leave to brew and drink when cold.

Barley

Barley seeds have been found in ancient tombs dating from 3,500 B.C.

American Indians and also settlers used barley water, hot or cold, as a treatment for children's diarrhoea, and to relieve fevers and stomach irritations. The juice can also be used as a compress to soothe tired eyes.

Preparation: Boil two ounces of pearl barley in a little water, strain and add the barley to four pints of boiling water and boil until reduced to two pints. Add lemon juice to taste and leave to cool. Take regular cupfuls throughout the day.

Beth Root

The root is the medicinal part, which was used by Native Americans, to reduce pain and difficulty of childbirth, hence its other common name 'Birth Root'.

Regular intake is thought to prevent bleeding from the nose, mouth, stomach, bowels and bladder.

Externally, it can be made into a poultice as an effective treatment for ulcers, insect stings and tumours.

Preparation: Make tea from one teaspoonful of the powdered root added to a cupful of boiling water left to stand until cool. Take a cupful two or three times a day.

Cardamom

Cardamom is a popular culinary spice, which is also used as a treatment for digestive disorders, especially wind and bloating.

In India it is called 'Queen of Spices' and is a traditional cure for hiccups, where two cardamoms are pounded and infused in a cupful of boiling water to which five mint leaves are added. The sufferer sips the drink while still hot.

The plant was introduced gradually to the West by spice traders, and soon it became one of the world's most highly prized spices and an important flavouring in food. In ancient Egypt it was valued as a breath freshener and as a whitener for the teeth.

Preparation: The parts used in tea are the fruits and seeds, of which two or three are added to each cupful of boiling water and left to stand five minutes or so before serving.

Celery Seed

The main parts used in medicine are root and seeds, which have featured in folk medicine for thousands of years, even in pre-Biblical times. It has featured in Chinese medicine since the 5th century B.C. and in ancient Egypt it was used to treat diseases cast by demons.

In modern day India the plant – called Ajmoda – is used to treat asthma, bronchitis, ailments of liver and spleen, urinary discharges, rheumatism, hiccups, flatulence, nasal catarrh and fever.

Celery is an excellent diuretic, and is also believed to have aphrodisiac qualities. An old saying suggests: 'If women knew what celery did to men, they would go and get some from Paris to Rome.'

During the Middle Ages the plant was also thought to help couples increase their chances of producing male children.

Celery tea benefits the kidneys, helping to flush out toxins and offer fast effective relief from cystitis. The juice is believed to induce delayed menstruation.

WARNING: Not to be taken by anyone suffering from kidney disease. Do not take during pregnancy. Unsuitable for children and not recommended for prolonged use.

Preparation: Add one teaspoonful of celery – seed or root – to each cupful of boiling water. Stir and leave to stand in the teapot for a few minutes. Serve hot.

Camomile

In olden times, the plant was thought to be particularly kind to women, as Harold Ward says in *Herbal Manual*: 'The famous camomile tea is taken for nervous and bilious headache, as an aid to digestion, and for hysterical tendencies in women.' Earl Mindell also refers to the many benefits for women, saying: 'Back in the days when women often came down with a mysterious malady called *the vapours*, a cup of camomile tea was often prescribed to relieve female anxiety.'

In ancient Rome the women took camomile tea to relieve period pains.

More recently, the herbalist Parkinson wrote: 'Camomile is put to diverse and sundry uses, both for pleasure and profit, both for the sick and the healthy, in bathing to comfort and strengthen the healthy, and to ease pain in the diseased.'

The tea can also be taken by children as a mild soporific. It helps calm over-active children and anyone suffering from anxiety. Romany families still consider the tea a powerful antidote to nightmares.

The tea is believed to control nervous twitches and shaking especially when honey is added. With or without honey, camomile tea makes an excellent gargle for sore throats, gingivitis and laryngitis. Used cold, the juice can be applied as a wash for tired eyes. It is also thought to offer relief from allergic reactions, either taken as tea or used as a wash over affected skin. The flowers, made into a paste, can be applied as a poultice to inflamed areas such as sores and swellings.

Externally, the flower heads can be made into a soothing lotion for toothache, earache and neuralgia. The tea can be added to bath water to reduce painful sunburn and to stop a tan turning patchy, as well as for relieving painful and irritating haemorrhoids.

Still today it is prescribed to ease premenstrual tension and painful periods, as well as symptoms of the menopause. Last, but not least, the wash can be applied liberally all over the body as a powerful repellent for mosquitoes and summer insects.

WARNING: The plant can be irritating to sensitive skin.

Preparation: Infuse two teaspoonfuls of flowers to each cupful of boiling water and leave in the teapot to brew for five to ten minutes.

Cinnamon

The plant comes originally from Sri Lanka and has been used for thousands of years as a culinary and medicinal herb. Its earliest known use was in Europe around five centuries B.C. King Solomon was also thought to recommend the herb, especially for weak digestion and biliousness.

The tea helps clear the mind and improve concentration, making this a useful pre-examination tonic. Cinnamon has a warming flavour making it a particularly effective treatment for sore throats, colds, influenza and poor circulation. It is also used to help stimulate the appetite.

Preparation: Add half teaspoonful of powdered cinnamon to each cupful of hot water and leave to stand in teapot until brewed. Add honey to improve the flavour.

Comfrey

Culpeper himself prescribed comfrey, saying: 'It is specially good for ruptures and broken bones, so powerful to consolidate and knit together, that if they be boiled with dissevered pieces of flesh in a pot, it will join them together.' This knitting function is considered by Mrs. M. Grieve who suggests the reason is the allantoin content (*A Modern Herbal*', published by Cape, London, 1931, reprinted in 1974).

In folk medicine the tea is given to anyone who feels below par, even without recognisable symptoms. It is beneficial for sufferers from arthritis and many digestive disorders.

The plant also contains essential vitamins and minerals, including some found in meat, making it a useful addition to the vegetarian diet.

Soak tired feet in hot water to which the tea is added. The treatment also helps to reduce the pain of arthritis and rheumatism. Allegedly, the plant offers major benefits for sufferers from warts as Dr. Krischner points out in *Nature's Healing Grasses:* 'Use it dry or as a wet mash on troublesome growths and oversize persistent body warts.'

Externally, apply it cold as a lotion for cuts and grazes and to help alleviate the pain of rashes, burns and swollen breasts, and to cool areas of painful sunburn.

WARNING: Controversy surrounds internal use of comfrey. Research has suggested that the herb may have caused cancer in rats. Excessive internal use must be avoided except under strict medical guidance.

Preparation: Add a teaspoonful of the herb to each cupful of boiling water and leave to stand in the teapot until thoroughly brewed.

Dandelion

Believed to have originated in Greece, dandelion can now be found growing freely all over the world.

It has extensive uses as a food and beverage. American Indians, for example, consider the plant vital to health and use it in food, tea and as a treatment for numerous ailments. Early records show it was used as a sedative in sixteenth-century Germany, while in France it is still a common ingredient in salads.

Root and leaves are used in folk medicine to treat numerous ailments when it is often taken hot as tea or cool as a healing juice.

Russians use the root prepared as an extract, which is added to vodka, tea or coffee and used to treat jaundice, skin irregularities and digestive troubles.

Herbalists through the ages have considered dandelion as one of nature's finest healers. Dandelion is rich in nutritive salts, which help purify the blood and destroy excess acid. Tea made from the leaves improves liver and kidney function. Dandelion is a powerful diuretic, helping to increase the flow of urine. The tea is particularly good at treating cystitis and other urinary problems. The French also use it as a soothing lotion for chronic skin complaints.

Preparation: For an infusion, take half a cupful of dandelion leaves and top with a pint of boiling water. Steep for half an hour, then drain and serve cold.

Echinacea

The plant is a particular favourite of the North American Indians who have used it as an internal and external medicine for numerous skin complaints, including snake bites, cuts and stings, and battle wounds. Today they apply the juice locally as a treatment for toothache and gum disorders.

Herbalists throughout the world prescribe a similar treatment for patients suffering from acne, eczema and boils. A recent survey amongst U.S. herbalists revealed that echinacea is one of the most important herbs of all.

The root is the medicinal part, commonly referred to as rhizome. Regular drinks are also thought to benefit the immune system and help keep the body healthy. In Germany some 150 proprietary medicines contain the herb, primarily for its effects on the immune system.

Hobbs (*Echinacea: The Immune Herb!*) says: 'Echinacea is probably one of the most promising immune ingredients and modulators, with numerous scientific studies and clinical evidence in its favour.'

The herb is particularly good as a treatment for colds and influenza, sinus congestion, sore throat, tonsillitis, neuralgia and shingles.

The cold tea makes a fine gargle for throat, mouth and gum disorders.

Preparation: Add two teaspoonfuls of the dried root to each cupful of boiling water and leave to stand in a teapot until brewed.

Elderflower

The flowers are the main parts used in tea, which is believed to cleanse the blood and benefit the immune function, helping the body resist infection and fight disease.

A lotion made from the leaves is an ancient remedy for chilblains.

One of the plant's main functions is in fighting conditions of the nose and airways, such as colds and influenza, nasal congestion and sinus problems.

Preparation: Add two teaspoonfuls of dried flowers to each cupful of boiling water and leave to stand in a teapot until fully brewed.

Fennel

Roman soldiers chewed fennel on long marches when they were unable to stop for food. In ancient times the plant was hung outside homes to protect against witches and demons.

The seeds are used as a treatment for digestive disorders and as a diuretic and appetite enhancer. The tea is also beneficial to some chest complaints, notably asthma. Herbalists administer fennel tea to sufferers from colic, indigestion and biliousness and to help increase milk flow in nursing mothers.

The plant has long been considered a potent aphrodisiac.

Its use as a treatment for many eye conditions, including conjunctivitis and eyestrain, may stem from observations that adders like fennel, supposedly rubbing their eyes hard against the plant to emit a juice which strengthens the eyesight!

For centuries the juice has been applied locally to joint inflammations caused by rheumatism and arthritis.

WARNING: The plant is thought to be phototoxic and can be damaging to sensitive skins.

Preparation: Add one teaspoonful of dried seeds to each cupful of boiling water and leave to stand in a teapot until thoroughly brewed.

Fenugreek

Use of the plant for medicine dates back to ancient times, when Hippocrates himself is believed to have prescribed it.

The herb is considered especially beneficial for women. In India, for instance, it has been used for centuries to increase milk flow in nursing mothers and in China it is used to control hot flushes associated with the menopause. Fenugreek tea makes a good treatment for colds and sinus congestion.

Specific treatments today are for digestive disorders and problems of the digestive tract.

The herb remains a popular folk remedy for sore throats and colds as well as being considered a powerful aphrodisiac. Research currently taking place in India shows fenugreek may also be useful against diabetes.

Externally, the juice helps relieve skin irritations and reduces the pain of neuralgia, swollen glands and other inflammations. As a gargle it helps fight soreness of the throat, mouth and gums.

WARNING: Not to be taken during pregnancy.

Preparation: Add one teaspoonful of the seeds to each cupful of boiling water and leave to stand in a teapot until fully brewed.

Feverfew

The tea is used in folk medicine to rid the lungs of phlegm and is also believed to relieve depression and melancholia.

Culpeper recommended the herb for women, reporting it a 'general strengthener of their wombs' and in both sexes 'very effectual for all pains in the head'. As a treatment for headache, Culpeper's view was shared by later herbalist, John Hill, who wrote: 'In the worst headache, this herb exceeds whatever else is known.'

In ancient and modern times the tea has emerged as a popular treatment for dizziness, migraine and sickness, especially when headache is present. At King's College in London patients suffering from migraine were recently administered the leaves over a period of several months.

Almost three-quarters found a reduction in severity and frequency of migraines, while the remainder noticed no appreciable difference.

Consumed as a tea and applied as a poultice the plant is commonly used to treat arthritis and rheumatism.

WARNING: Not to be taken by children or during pregnancy.

Preparation: Add two large teaspoonfuls of the crushed leaves to each cupful of boiling water and leave to stand in a teapot until brewed. Take several times a day while the condition lasts and take daily to help prevent migraines from occurring.

Ginger

The Chinese have used ginger for medicinal and culinary purposes for more than two thousand years. The Japanese also consider it has major healing benefits, especially for cleaning the palate and treating digestive disorders.

Early 20th-century practitioners of the American Physio-Medical School found the root was directly beneficial to the uterus and often prescribed it for chronic nervous fatigue.

Herbalist Ellingwood said of ginger: 'This agent is mentioned in but few therapeutic works, although it occupies an important place, and should not be neglected. It is a profound and immediate stimulant, an active diaphoretic, an anodyne in gastric and intestinal pain, and a sedative to an irritated and overwrought system when there is extreme exhaustion.'

The plant is also believed to have aphrodisiac qualities. Jerome Cardan said of ginger: 'It helps a lustful nature' and for thousands of years it has been added to drinks to excite the senses and allegedly improve the sex drive.

Many species of ginger exist, according to habitat. The root is the main part used in medicine to treat minor and longer-lasting ailments.

Take the tea to improve the appetite. Taken hot, the tea helps induce delayed menstruation as well as offering relief from severe menstrual cramps. It is also used extensively to treat morning and motion sickness.

Research suggests ginger tea may help the heart stay healthy. A study published in the *New England Journal of Medicine* (1980) says it may help reduce cholesterol levels, possibly by restricting the amount of cholesterol absorbed by the blood.

Added to bath water the tea helps fight colds and influenza and is particularly welcoming for those who work out of doors in cold weather.

WARNING: Used to excess ginger can irritate the skin and digestive tract.

Preparation: Add the crushed root to boiling water, amount according to taste.

Golden Seal (Sometimes 'Goldenseal')

In earlier times liquid from the plant was used as an external and internal treatment for gonorrhoea and syphilis. Today we are more likely to administer it as an antidote to 'flu and sinus congestion, or to treat constipation and to alleviate haemorrhoids.

Tea made from the root helps cleanse the system but should be avoided by anyone suffering from high blood pressure.

Specific treatments using the plant include catarrh, indigestion and heartburn, loss of appetite, haemorrhoids, enteritis, cystitis and sore throat.

In America's Deep South herbalists use the tea as a heart tonic, to reduce mouth and throat ulcers and as a treatment for ringworm and other intestinal parasites.

Lemon Balm

Lemon balm is a relaxant and is used in folk medicine as a treatment for stress and nervous exhaustion.

It has a long history as a rejuvenating herb. For example, *The London Dispensary* (1696) says of it: 'As essence of balm given every morning will restore youth, strengthen the brain, relieve languishing nature and prevent baldness.'

Culpeper, too, used lemon balm, testifying: 'Let a syrup made with the juice of it and sugar be kept in every gentle woman's house to relieve the weak stomachs and sick bodies of their poor and sickly neighbours.'

Modern day herbalists still administer the herb as a treatment for stomach upsets, nervous exhaustion and tension.

Externally the tea can be applied as a compress to relieve painful cold sores.

Preparation: Make an infusion from two teaspoonfuls of the dried herb – fresh leaves are best – added to a cupful of warm water, left to stand until cool.

Limeflower

Limeflower is an age-old remedy for nervous conditions and as a stimulant. Modern day French and Germans use the tea to benefit digestion and induce sound sleep.

It also helps prevent and reduce painful headaches and migraine as well as being an effective treatment for colds and influenza.

Preparation: Make an infusion from two teaspoonfuls of flower added to a cupful of hot water. Strain and take hot several times a day.

Marigold

The ancient Romans noted that marigold flowered on the first day of the month and named it *Calendula officinalis*.

Culpeper and other early herbalists used it to treat depression and low morale and it was also used extensively to reduce sweating caused by fevers at the onset of serious illness, notably measles and smallpox.

The tea is commonly used in folk medicine to treat cramps, poor digestion and ulcers of the stomach. Some modern day herbalists report useful feedback for it being a possible treatment for the debilitating condition known as M.E.

Marigold has a long history as a healing herb. In 1901, W. Hale White, M.D., F.R.C.P., lecturer in medicine at London's Guy's Hospital said of marigold, it 'decreases odour, cleans surfaces, relieves pain and promotes repair.'

Toothache is one such pain the plant can relieve, *as The Garden's Labyrinth* (1577) reveals: 'The juice of marigold petals mixed with vinegar to be rubbed on gums and teeth becomes a sovereign remedy for the assuaging of the grievous pain of the teeth.'

The tea makes an excellent mouth wash and also helps reduce fever by stimulating sweating. It is a detoxifying and cleansing drink.

Made into a lotion with apple cider vinegar the juice brings comfort to sprains and other areas of painful inflammation.

Externally, the tea also makes a powerful lotion for treating burns, wounds and bruises and can be used as an eyewash for conjunctivitis. The juice was used extensively on the battlefield during the First World War to clean wounds and fight infection.

It has always been considered a good skin tonic; even Henry VIII used it, saying: 'This tea, if it is taken before the pimples do appear, then it will heal the sick person with God's Grace.'

Preparation: Add one or two teaspoonfuls of dried flowers to a cupful of boiling water and leave to cool.

Marshmallow

Marshmallow has been used as medicine for centuries. In ancient Greece the root was soaked in wine and administered as a treatment for dry stubborn coughs. During his reign (A.D. 742-814), King Charlemagne ruled that the plant be grown throughout his lands.

Even Culpeper used it, saying: 'You may remember that not long since there was a raging disease called the bloody flux – the College of Physicians not knowing what to make of it, called it The Plague in the Guts, for they were not too enlightened about it . . . My son was taken with the same disease; myself being in the country I was sent for; the only thing I gave him to drink was mallow bruised and boiled both in milk; in two days it cured him, and I have here to show my thankfulness to God in communicating it to his creatures, leaving it to posterity.'

Today the tea is administered as a treatment for constipation, cystitis and breathing problems.

Preparation: Add one teaspoonful of leaves – dried or fresh – to each cupful of boiling water. Leave to stand in the teapot until thoroughly brewed.

Mullein

The seeds are a powerful treatment for insomnia as testified by the activities of poachers who used to sprinkle ponds with mullein seeds to tranquillise fish who, obligingly, fell asleep and floated to the surface.

The tea is believed to relieve congestion of the lungs and is also used to calm nerves and induce sound sleep. As a treatment for insomnia, add a teaspoonful of seeds to a cupful of hot milk and take just before going to bed. Regular intake is frequently prescribed to sufferers from ulcers and colitis. The warm juice is also believed to ease painful piles when applied locally using a clean cloth.

Preparation: A handful of leaves, boiled in a quart of water, can be strained and the warm juice and applied to swollen glands for fast, effective relief.

Nettle

Nettle is another plant with a long and fascinating history as a healing herb, especially among Native Americans who use the branches to soothe pain, literally by striking the affected parts with the branches. Early and modern tribes use a decoction of the root as a bathing fluid for rheumatic pains and stiffness of the joints. As a poultice, the pounded leaves are used throughout the world as a dressing for painful swellings and stiffness.

Hippocrates himself used nettles in medicine and as a health-giving food.

The tea is also prescribed to combat allergy, especially when nose and chest are congested. In a recent study carried out at the American National College of Naturopathic Medicine, over half the patients who took part in the study said that nettle had proved extremely beneficial in relieving their allergy symptoms.

Other ailments said to benefit from regular intake of nettle tea include asthma, arthritis, gout, kidney disorders and digestive system problems. It is also thought to increase the flow of milk in nursing mothers and is frequently prescribed for vaginal infections such as thrush and to help regulate menstrual flow.

Russians are particularly fond of using nettles in herbal medicines, believing it is a powerful antiseptic, astringent and blood purifier. Externally, the tea can be massaged into the scalp to help stimulate hair growth.

WARNING: Nettle tea increases blood pressure and should not be taken by anyone suffering from high blood pressure.

Preparation: An infusion can be made from two teaspoonfuls of dried leaves added to a cupful of boiling water. Strain and take hot or cold.

Parsley

The medicinal parts are the leaves, root and seeds, in short the entire plant!

The Russian equivalent, Petrushka, is used extensively in food and medicine; preparations of tea and juice are being used to treat dropsy, kidney and bladder infections, liver and spleen ailments, and to bring rapid relief from painful prostate. Regular intake of tea keeps the breath fresh and healthy and is also thought to benefit allergy sufferers.

Parsley tea is a mild diuretic and helps alleviate bloating and water retention. Modern herbalists also administer the juice to regulate menstruation. Externally, the juice can be applied as an insect repellent.

WARNING: Not to be taken during pregnancy.

Preparation: Add one teaspoonful of crushed parsley to each cupful of boiling water and leave to stand in the teapot until thoroughly brewed.

Peppermint

The tea can be used to treat flatulence and disorders of the gastrointestinal tract. It is particularly good for relieving period pains, irritable bowel syndrome and palpitations. Research suggests drinking peppermint tea reduces the time the food takes to travel through the body and relaxes the stomach muscles.

Peppermint tea makes an excellent gargle for sore throats and can be added to the evening bath water to induce sound sleep.

Give small sips of peppermint tea to children suffering from travel sickness or soak a clean handkerchief in strong peppermint tea and let the child sniff it during the journey.

Earl Mindell *(The Herb Bible)* considers peppermint one of the best treatments for headache, suggesting: 'For a headache, try a strong cup of peppermint tea and lie down for fifteen to twenty minutes. I think that it works better than aspirin or paracetamol.'

WARNING: The plant can cause irritation to sensitive skin. Not to be taken during pregnancy.

Preparation: Add two teaspoonfuls of peppermint to each cupful of boiling water and leave to stand in the teapot until thoroughly brewed. Take three or four times a day.

Raspberry

Modern day Romany families tell how travelling women often used to pull their caravans into a lay-by while they gave birth and within an hour they were back on the road again. The reason for such fast and painless childbirth among gypsy women was that they began taking regular drinks of raspberry tea as soon as they learned they were pregnant. Raspberry foliage is rich in iron and is thought to benefit many areas of the reproductive process, from sterility to morning sickness, as well as shortening labour and easing delivery.

In America's Deep South the tea is administered to strengthen the uterus and help prevent miscarriages, as well as to increase the flow of milk in nursing mothers.

Preparation: Make a juice from the crushed berries watered to taste. Or make a tea from one teaspoonful of fresh leaves added to each cupful of boiling water and leave to stand in the teapot until thoroughly brewed.

Red Clover

Early herbalists consider red clover one of the most important contents of the medicine chest, even considering it a potential antidote to cancer, although this has not been thoroughly substantiated by modern day scientists.

Early herbalist Fernie says of the plant: 'The likelihood is that whatever virtue the red clover can boast for counter-acting a scrofulous disposition, and as antidote to cancer, resides in its highly-elaborated lime, silica, and other earthy salts.'

As a gargle, red clover brings fast relief to sore throats and mouth infections. The cold tea or juice can be applied direct to areas of rectal and vaginal irritation.

Taken as a drink or used as a lotion the herb helps clear numerous skin complaints. The tea cleanses the body and helps fight infection.

Preparation: Make a tea by adding one dessertspoonful of crushed leaves and flowers to a cupful of boiling water and leave to steep for at least thirty minutes. Take several times a day.

Rose

Tea made from fresh rose petals can be used as an inhalation to help relieve sinus congestion and to induce sound sleep. Rose tea is used by North American Indians as a treatment for morning sickness.

Rose in many forms is believed to benefit patients suffering from anxiety and nerves. According to Daniel Ryman *(Aromatherapy: The Encyclopaedia of Plants and Oils and How They Help You):* 'Rose essential oil is good for people with a very nervous disposition. It seems to work on the nervous system, calming the patient and is better received by women than men. Massage oil into the solar plexus; apply diluted oil after a bath and drink rose petal infusions. Rose also helps insomnia.'

Preparation: Add a handful of fresh crushed rose petals to every cupful of boiling water and leave to stand in the teapot until thoroughly brewed.

Rosemary

Rosemary was mentioned in the early writings of Pliny, Dioscordes and early Arab physicians.

In the early thirteenth century, the Queen of Hungary was said to have been cured of paralysis by continued applications of rosemary juice to her affected limbs. The formula for 'Queen of Hungary Water', hand-written by the Queen herself, is housed in the Imperial Library in Vienna.

Much later, Culpeper says it is good for 'diseases of the head and brain, as the giddiness and swimming therein', hence the reason today's herbalists administer rosemary for dizziness caused by disturbances of the inner ear.

The tea stimulates the flow of bile from the gall bladder and is believed to stimulate the thought processes and keep the memory sharp, even in advanced old age. Students in ancient Greece took rosemary to improve their memory, while for others regular internal and external application was thought to help keep the body young. Applied to the scalp it is used to treat dandruff and other scaly conditions. The juice has always been considered a powerful eye tonic, of which Culpeper wrote: 'It helps dim eyes, and procures a clear sight.'

In America's Deep South the tea is used as a treatment for insomnia. Today, athletes and runners say the tea, rubbed into the muscles, helps prevent muscular strain. Throughout the world it is considered a powerful treatment for headaches and migraine, especially where caused by anxiety and tension.

As an alleged aphrodisiac, the plant is believed to work on the nerve centres and activate circulation of the blood. Seventeenth-century French noblewoman Mme. de Sauvigne, wrote about rosemary telling her daughter: 'I use it every day to become inebriated, I always have some handy.'

WARNING: Avoid during pregnancy.

Preparation: Make an infusion from one teaspoonful of dried rosemary to a cupful of boiling water. Take three times a day.

Sage

Sage has a long history as a healing herb as the old English proverb shows: 'He that would live for aye must eat sage in May.'

Sixteenth-century herbalist, Gerard, believed sage 'quickens the senses and memory, strengthening the sinews and restoring health to those suffering from palsies and trembling of limbs'. Culpeper prescribed the tea as a mouthwash for sore gums.

American Indians use sage tea as a rubdown particularly for patients suffering from fever. Coupled with apple cider vinegar, the treatment is particularly beneficial and is commonly prescribed in most areas of folk medicine. Hot sage tea induces perspiration and can be helpful in overcoming fever.

The leaves are the medicinal part and are often used in gargles for keeping the breath fresh and the teeth clean and healthy.

Sometimes called the 'thinker's tea', sage allegedly improves the thought processes and is often used to help clear the mind in students undergoing examinations.

Sage tea is used throughout the world to treat gastric debility, flatulence and as a gargle for soreness of the throat and mouth, oral thrush, gingivitis and laryngitis.

WARNING: Not to be taken during pregnancy or while breast-feeding.

Preparation: Add two teaspoonfuls of crushed sage to one pint of boiling water, steep for an hour and strain. Take hot as a tea or cold as a juice.

Saw Palmeto

The herb is a particular favourite of North American Indians who use it as a sedative, diuretic, expectorant, tonic and nutritive. Like many aboriginal tribes they also believe it cures impotency as well as being a powerful aphrodisiac. Herbalists still prescribe the herb for 'honeymoon cystitis', the result of excessive sexual activity among newlyweds. In Germany saw palmetto goes into many proprietary drugs for problems of the prostate.

The juice is believed to improve muscle tone and help fight colds, bronchitis and asthma.

On its Internet home page, Herbal Resources Inc. has this to say about the herb: 'Saw palmetto is a herb that acts to tone and strengthen the male reproductive system. It may be used with safety where a boost to the male sex hormones is required. It is specific in cases of enlarged prostate glands.'

Preparation: Make a tea or juice from the crushed berries with water added to taste.

Slippery Elm

The plant grows in many parts of the United States and Canada where it is a favourite of native tribes.

Herbalists have used it throughout the ages, including Kloss who recommends it as a suppository for vaginal problems *(Back to Eden)*.

Tea made from the inner bark offers fast effective pain relief from post gastro-enteritis, minor stomach upsets, indigestion and heartburn, minor wounds and some skin conditions. Some herbalists administer it to relieve the pain of gastric ulcers.

Preparation: Add two teaspoonfuls of the dried inner bark to each cupful of boiling water and leave to stand in the teapot until thoroughly brewed.

Strawberry Leaf

The tea is mildly astringent and diuretic and is used as a purifier for the blood of patients suffering from minor and serious skin conditions such as psoriasis, eczema and extreme dryness.

It can also be consumed regularly as a treatment for diarrhoea, dysentery, weakness of the intestines, and urinary infections.

Externally, juice or tea can be applied to mild burns and minor skin conditions. Wrung out on a cloth it helps clear oily skin, pimples and eczema.

Preparation: Add one teaspoonful of the fresh or dried herb to each cupful of boiling water and leave to stand for fifteen minutes. Strain and serve hot or cold.

Thyme

The whole plant has been used in medicines since ancient times, even by Culpeper who states: 'It is under the dominion of Venus and under the sign of Aries and therefore chiefly appropriated to the head.'

For generations, herbalists have used thyme to help overcome shyness. Gerard claimed thyme was beneficial 'against the ramblings and gripping of the belly'.

The plant was considered useful in helping eliminate phlegm without side-effects or discomfort, according to Culpeper: 'It is so harmless, you need not fear the use of it.'

More recently, Mrs. Grieve writing in *A Modern Herbal* lists the following uses of thymoil (oil of thyme):

'As an antiseptic lotion and mouthwash; as a paint in ringworm, in eczema, psoriasis, broken chilblains, parasitic skin affections and burns; as an ointment, half-strength, perfumed with lavender, to keep off gnats and mosquitoes . . . It is most useful given in large doses, to robust adults; in capsules, as a worming ingredient, to expel parasites, especially the miner's worm; and it has also been used for diabetes and bladder stones.'

Specific ailments for which the tea is administered include water retention and bloating, colds and stubborn coughs, asthma, mouth and throat infections, loss of appetite, sluggish digestion, nervous exhaustion and depression. Mixed with honey the juice can be taken in small doses, several times a day, to ease a sore throat and post nasal drip.

Its diuretic action particularly benefits cases of gout, arthritis, muscular aches and pains and build-up of uric acid.

The tea is especially good for soothing sore throats as well as a treatment for common colds and influenza. It is often used to treat hysteria, headache, nervous disorders and dizziness.

Add to bath water to help relieve painful arthritis and rheumatism.

Preparation: An infusion can be made from one teaspoonful of thyme to a cupful of boiling water left to stand for half an hour. Drain and serve hot or cold.

Valerian

Being a natural sedative, valerian tea is a common treatment for people suffering from nerves and anxiety. Earl Mindell refers to the plant as 'the valium of the nineteenth century'.

For its tranquillising effects, it was used extensively during the Blitz in England during the Second World War and is still prescribed today as a sedative. It also helps to reduce muscle spasms and relieve melancholy.

Today, the plant is considered one of the safest of all natural medicines and in Germany more than one hundred over-the-counter treatments contain valerian. Top level research even indicates the herb is as effective as some sleeping pills in promoting sound sleep.

On its Internet home page, Herbal Resources Inc. has this to say about valerian: 'The research into valerian is confirming the traditional experience of the herbalist. In one study, valerian produced a significant decrease in subjectively evaluated sleep scores and an improvement in sleep quality. Improvement was most notably amongst those who considered themselves poor or irregular sleepers and smokers.'

Mixed with ginger the tea is particularly warming and helps stimulate the circulation.

Valerian tea is a common treatment for insomnia, pre-menstrual tension, nervous conditions and panic attacks.

Externally, the lotion can be used to treat eczema.

Preparation: To make tea, add one teaspoonful of the dried root to a cupful of cold water.

Verbena

The Druids considered verbena as one of the most sacred herbs and used it to treat many conditions.

Coffin, writing in the mid-nineteenth century says that verbena is 'one of the strongest sweating medicines in nature. It is good for colds, coughs and pain in the head, and some years ago it was highly esteemed as a remedy for consumption . . . Verbena relieves teething discomfort in children; it also destroys worms. Administered as a tea, it reduces the pains of labour; as a diuretic it increases the urinary discharge.'

The French are particularly fond of the tea and consider it a great tonic packed with cleansing and toning properties and being particularly kind on the liver.

It is a powerful digestive tonic and helps reduce the pain caused by gallstones.

Preparation: Add an ounce of the dried herb to one pint of boiling water and leave to steep for half an hour before straining, then serve cold.

Bibliography and Recommended Reading

Herbal Medicine by Dian Dincin Buchman, published by Tiger.

Off-The-Shelf Natural Health by Mark Mayell, published by Boxtree.

The Herb Bible by Earl Mindell, published by Vermilion.

Echinacea: The Immune Herb! by Christopher Hobbs, published by Botanica Press.